The Life and Times of
Charlie Chaplin

The Life and Times of
Charlie Chaplin

Nandini Saraf

Ocean Books Pvt. Ltd.
ISO 9001:2015 Publishers

Published by
Ocean Books (P) Ltd.
4/19 Asaf Ali Road,
New Delhi-110 002 (INDIA)
e-mail: info@oceanbooks.in

ISBN 978-81-8430-208-0
The Life and Times of Charlie Chaplin
by Nandini Saraf

Edition
2021

Price
₹ 250.00 (Rupees Two Hundred Fifty only)

Printed at
Narula Printers, Delhi

Dedicated to
My Father, Mother,
Sister and Brother

Contents

Charlie Chaplin, the Silent Tramp

The man, who began his career in the movie business, when film-making was just another medium of entertainment, brought with him a revolution, to such effect that the film became an art form through which artists started expressing themselves – which was once thought to be the job of only a playwright or an author.

Charlie Chaplin is indeed the best silent comedian that the Cinema has ever had. Miming was not an unheard form of art when Charlie started with it; but he had a talent, which others could barely match up to.

His is a story which in itself made another movie, named *Chaplin* that was released in 1992; this film made the new generation see him in a new light, and it was one of the biggest tributes that he could have ever got.

After knowing Charlie's story, one could only wonder – such was his humility, that even after having lived through a childhood of extreme poverty, he was still a very modest man when he became one of the highest paid artists in the Film Industry.

Charlie has acted in films, directed them, and even composed a few musical scores for his films. This multi-talented artist has won over a million hearts, who are all thankful to him to have made them smile even during the acute times of the war.

Charlie has appeared in more than eighty films throughout the fifty-plus years of his career; and each of these films have managed to gain a large audience, sometimes, just to watch him.

Today, his name has become a legend; he is that comedian, who through his comedies said a lot more than one could grasp; whose actions alone spoke everything that one would have wanted to know. His famous character of the Tramp was a 'foil' to the society, which illustrated the futility of its pretentiousness.

Thomas Burke's description of this great man is most peculiar. He painted a beautiful picture of Charlie through these following words, "A frail figure, small footed, and with hands as exquisite as those of Madame la Marquise—a mass of brindled-gray hair above a face of high colour and nervous features. In conversation the pale hands flash and flutter and the eyes twinkle; the body sways and swings, and the head darts birdlike back and forth, in time with the soft chanting voice. His personality is as volatile as his lithe and resilient figure. He has something of Hans Andersen, of Ariel, touched with rumours of far-off fairyland tears. But something more than pathos is here. Almost, I would say, he is a tragic figure."[1]

Now, before divulging further into the life of Charlie Chaplin, the author would like to say a few words regarding the medium which had made him so famous.

❑

The Age of the Silent Moving Pictures

The first moving picture ever to be recorded was in 1878, when Eadweard Muybridge captured a galloping horse. He was working for Leland Stanford of Stanford University, who was trying to prove a scientific question of whether all four hooves of a horse are off the ground while it is running. Muybridge used a number of cameras for this activity and then arranged all the pictures in a series to create the effect of a moving picture.

Hereafter, everything that happened is a long history of how Moving Pictures became not just a medium to keep records, but an Art Form for commercial purposes. Thomas Alva Edison, along with his assistant William K. Laurie Dickson, developed a *Kinetoscope* which could help the general public to view a moving picture individually through a peephole viewer window situated at the top of the device. By 1892, Edison had produced various movies on 35 mm films and wanted to show them to the people. Hence, on April 14, 1894, the first paid exhibition of the moving picture was set up in New York. Edison did not believe that moving pictures had any future for a large-scale audience and, therefore, thought that his device would rather help him gather more profits.

It was on December 28, 1895, that Lumiere Brothers first showcased their moving picture on a large screen to an audience in Paris. The excitement of the people was incomparable. Before this, they had only seen still photographs of actual happenings, but now they were viewing an event as it happened even without being at that place. This was definitely phenomenal.

Along with Edison and Lumiere Brothers, there were other companies like David Wark Griffith's 'The Biograph Company' and 'The Georges Melies Company' who were also producing movies. Griffith's *The Birth of a Nation* (1915) was the most popular silent movie of all times and Melies was the pioneer for horror, science fiction and dark comedy movies.

Special mention is to be made of Edwin Stanton Porter, who was Edison's employee and used to direct most of his films. In the early 1900s, he produced a few noteworthy movies like *Life of an American Fireman* (1902), *The Great Train Robbery* (1903) and *The Kleptomaniac* (1905).

Silent comedies, of which Charlie Chaplin is the most celebrated star, came into existence from the second decade of the twentieth century. Charlie entered the film arena in 1913, when Mack Sennet of Keystone Film Company hired him, during which time he was in America for a tour with the Fred Karno comedy group. Back in London, he was already a popular name for his stage performances as a comedian.

Charlie Chaplin, along with other names such as Douglas Fairbanks, Mary Pickford, Tom Mix, Theda Bara, Lillian Gish, Edna Purviance and a few more, had become the face of the silent movies during the Great Depression and people found solace in watching them. Their movies were particularly popular among the general public because of the themes that they presented.

Then there came a time when many thought that it was time for the silent era to end. And thus arrived in the late 1920s, the '*talkies*' – movies that have synchronised sound. *Don Juan* (1926) was the first sound film produced under 'Warner Brothers' and the first film to have synchronised dialogues was *The Jazz Singer* (1927).

The following is an extract that was published in an article in the magazine *Illustrated World* in 1922. It criticised the silent movies and voiced its opinion on the need for talking pictures.

"The industry, while already a giant in size and accomplishment, has been permitted only half expression, only half development. But with the radio to act as its tongue, its handicapping lack of speech will be removed.

That industry is, of course, the movies. Speechless, it has perfected the art of visual expression to a degree that has won it the unqualified respect and affection of the entire human race....

Through all its progress its sponsors have mourned its handicaps; have irked under the inevitable burden of its muteness. Now they are eagerly awaiting the hour when the stifling hand of silence is lifted. They are certain that hour is coming, borne on the wings of the radio."[2]

But Charlie was not ready for this change. He did not believe in the talking when acting could do the job better; as he once said, "I do not have much patience with a thing of beauty that must be explained to be understood. If it does need additional interpretation by someone other than the creator, then I question whether it has fulfilled its purpose."

Similar were the thoughts of D.W. Griffith, who also said, "It is my arrogant belief that we have lost beauty."

Gerald Mast, the author of *The Comic Mind: Comedy and the Movies* (1979) had a balanced view on the silent movies, although he also spoke in support of the talkies. An extract from his book reads as follows: "The great silent movies revolve around the body and the personality of its owner; the great sound comedies revolve about structure and style – what happens, how it happens, and the way those happenings are depicted. Film comedy, as well as film art in general, was born from delight in physical movement. The essence of early film-making was to take some object (animate or inanimate) and simply watch it move.... The sound comedy is far more literary. Given the opportunity to use the essential tool of literature, words, as an intrinsic part of the film's conception, the filmmaker did not hesitate to do so. In silent films, the use of words in titles was intrusive, a deliberate interruption of the cinematic medium and a substitution of the literary one. We stop looking and start reading. But the sound film provided the means to watch the action and listen to the words at the same time. Whereas the silent performer was a physical being...the sound performer was both physical and intellectual at once."

People can argue for long, about both styles, but that does not diminish the art of Silent Movies and definitely not that of Charlie Chaplin.

Thus, it is now time to move on and talk solely about him.

❑

Early Years

Some people still might have the notion that Charlie Chaplin was an American, for his association with the American Cinema; as even the Prince of Wales had once asked him whether he was an American, to which he had subtly replied that he was English.

Charlie was born as Charles Spencer Chaplin, on April 16, 1889, in London to Charles and Hannah Chaplin, who were truly English by origin. Charlie also had an elder half-brother named Sydney Chaplin.

Several of his biographies claim that his place of birth is Kennington, although in his book, *My Autobiography*, he has mentioned it as East Lane, Walworth, and that his family later shifted to Kennington, a part of Lambeth, in South London.

An extract from the 'Introduction' given by David Robinson in *My Autobiography* reads as, "Chapter One begins in forthright Victorian biographical style: 'I was born on 16 April 1889, at eight o' clock at night, in East Lane Walworth.' When *My Autobiography* appeared in 1964, this was itself a revelation. The hundreds of books that had been devoted to Chaplin had vaguely placed his birth here, there and everywhere (even Fontainebleau), and no birth certificate exists to settle the question."[3]

Therefore, we take Charlie's word for it.

Not much is known about Charlie's father except that he was a performer in the Canterbury Music Hall where they often used to go to watch him play out various characters from a variety of English Dramas. He could also sing very well and had good knowledge of music. The senior Chaplin had also once got an opportunity to perform in the New York Theatre for which he had to leave London for a while.

Charlie's mother describes him as "a vaudevillian,[4] a quiet, brooding man with dark eyes." In his autobiography, he recalls, "Mother said he looked like Napoleon. He had a light baritone voice and was considered a very fine artist."[5]

Charles Sr. and Hannah had known each other since their teenage and were quite fond of each other. But at the age of eighteen, Hannah ran away with a middle-aged man to Africa, where she claimed to have spent a life of luxury. Soon after Sydney was born, she left her husband and came back to London. She then married Charles, who also adopted Sydney and gave him his name.

Charlie was born three years after their marriage and when he was only one year old, they got separated. His mother told him that the reason was his father's addiction to alcohol. Some speculate that it was because Hannah had an affair and got pregnant with Music Hall singer, Leo Dryden's child. A few months later, she gave birth to Wheeler Dryden whom his father took away when he was only six months old.

Charles and Hannah's children were mere minors and she had to take care of them both on her own, which goes without saying was quite a difficult task. She later sued Charles for non-support but that didn't help her much.

There is not much known about Charlie's ancestors except that his maternal grandfather, Hannah's father, was an Irish cobbler, who later settled in Kennington. And one of his grandmothers[6] was half gypsy, because of which many of his biographers speculate that his miming skills come from being of gypsy origin. Here is an extract from *Charlie Chaplin: His Life and Art* (1931) written by W. Dodgson Bowman which verifies this fact: "Some writers assert that he has gypsy blood in his veins. The writer of a book on *Travels in Spain* was greatly struck by the number of men he met in that country who seemed to be counterparts of Charlie, and wondered if his mimic gifts were inherited from dons or grandees."[7]

Hannah also had a sister, whom Charlie refers to as Aunt Kate in his autobiography, and says he did not know much about her, except that she used to visit then sometimes.

Hannah Chaplin was a performer on stage, mainly as a musician, and used to be a prominent part of Gilbert and Sullivan operas and other notable music plays of those times. When she was sixteen, she played the leading role in an Irish melodrama, *Shamus O' Brien*, in which Charles Sr. also played a part.

Charlie described her mother as having "fair complexion, violet-blue eyes and long brown hair". And later, some people told him that she was an attractive and charming lady.

After Charlie's father left them, Hannah started experiencing a downfall in her career. Her voice began to break and that often affected her performances. That day wasn't far when she had to leave her job.

Gradually, Hannah lost every penny that she had saved. She sold off her jewellery, her theatre clothes and all the valuables that she had ever possessed. Even when she had that job, it could not suffice for their livelihood. Now there were times when they did not even have enough for a proper meal. As a result, both her sons were somewhat malnourished and could not get much education.

What the children failed to notice at this time was that Hannah's own health had started deteriorating. In taking care of her children, she often slept empty stomach and the worry kept her mentally disturbed.

They shifted to a smaller place which only had one room. Hannah even stopped seeing her theatre friends as she was much embarrassed. Soon she took to sewing, as she was good at it, having stitched all her theatre clothes when she worked there.

But that too wasn't paying off well and didn't last long because her sewing machine had to be taken away due to non-payment of instalments. Meanwhile, Charlie's father also stopped paying regularly for the support of his children.

It was too much for them to bear and, therefore, the three of them took another drastic step.

In the autobiography, Charlie talks about his life in the Lambeth workhouse where all three of them got enrolled after they were completely broke. "Although we were aware of the shame of going to the workhouse, when Mother told us about it, both Sydney and I thought it adventurous and a change from living in one stuffy room. But on that doleful day, I didn't realize what was happening until we actually entered the workhouse gate. Then the forlorn bewilderment of it struck me; for there we were made to separate, Mother going in one direction to the woman's ward and we in another to the children's."[8]

Three weeks later, both the boys were admitted to Hanwell School for Orphans and Destitute Children, which was about twelve miles away from London. Charlie was much saddened by the recollection of this part of his life as he had to stay away from his mother. He was only six years old when he started going to that school.

During their stay at the school, their mother could only come to visit him once or twice as it wasn't allowed for her to leave the workhouse.

Sydney was now eleven years old, being four years elder to Charlie. As a rule of Hanwell, he had to leave for his training and he chose to go to Exmouth. Charlie was now alone at school but he somehow managed to study even though he never had any interest in it. As he points out in his autobiography, "Education bewildered me with knowledge and facts in which I was only mildly interested. If only someone had used salesmanship, had read a stimulating preface to each study that could have titillated my mind, infused me with fancy instead of facts, amused and intrigued me with the legerdemain of numbers, romanticized maps, given me a point of view about history and taught me the music of poetry, I might have been a scholar."[9]

These lines show how differently Charlie looked at education. It was as if he wanted a trailer for his subjects just like people are attracted toward watching movies after having a preview of it.

Charlie's stay at Hanwell was not for long. An epidemic of Ringworm broke out in the school and many were infected. Among them was Charlie. Hannah came to visit him during his sickness and he was too happy to see her. She told him about how she was trying to save up for a new house. This obviously excited him.

When Sydney came back from Exmouth, both of them left the school and went to stay with their mother. They were now staying in a room at Kennington Park. But this set up was not for long. They had to return to the workhouse because they still could not manage for the rent or for food. Charlie's father had stopped paying anything for them as he was suffering from alcoholism and could not work anymore; and as a result, Charlie's little family was broke again.

This time they went to a different workhouse and from there to Norwood Schools, which Charlie describes as less exciting than Hanwell.

It was during this time that their mother was first declared as insane and was sent to Cane Hill lunatic asylum. This news was given to Charles by Sydney, and it came to him as a shock. "When he told me I could not believe it. I did not cry, but a baffling despair overcame me. Why had she done this? Mother, so light-hearted and gay, how could she go insane?"[10]

The court now ordered both the brothers to stay at their father's house in Kennington Road, which somewhat excited Charlie. His father was living with another woman named Louise and they both had a son together. Charlie has not mentioned his name in the autobiography and neither has any other biographer in particular. But what one knows for sure is that Charlie's father did not ever marry Louise.

While they were staying with their father, both the brothers were sent to Kennington Road School. Charlie accounts in the autobiography that Louise did not treat them well and, therefore, he started loving to spend more time at school. "Saturday was a half-holiday, but I never looked forward to it because it meant going home and scrubbing floors and cleaning knives, and on that day, Louise invariably started drinking..... I was not yet eight years old, but those days were the longest and saddest of my life."[11]

Then one day Hannah arrived at their doorstep after being released from the asylum. She had come to take back her sons. Charlie was only too happy to meet her.

They were now staying in a room situated on a street behind Kennington Cross. His father too had started paying for them, and Hannah started with her needlework again.

Charlie's Many Talents

Charlie's first performance on stage was when he was only five years old. It was also the last night of his mother's career as a music hall singer. Charlie gives a vivid description of the night in these words, "Mother usually brought me to the theatre at night in preference to leaving me alone in rented rooms. She was playing the Canteen at Aldershot at the time, a grubby, mean theatre catering mostly to soldiers. They were a rowdy lot and wanted little excuse to deride and ridicule. To performers, Aldershot was a week of terror.

I remember standing in the wings when Mother's voice cracked and went into a whisper. The audience began to laugh and sing falsetto and to make catcalls. It was all vague and I did not quite understand what was going on. But the noise increased until Mother was obliged to walk off the stage. When she came into the wings, she was very upset and argued with the stage manager who, having seen me perform before Mother's friends, said something about letting me go on in her place.

And in the turmoil, I remember him leading me by the hand and, after a few explanatory words to the audience, leaving me on the stage alone. And before a glare of footlights and faces in smoke, I started to sing, accompanied by the orchestra, which fiddled about until it found my key....

Half-way through, a shower of money poured on to the stage. Immediately, I stopped and announced that I would pick up the money first and sing afterwards. This caused much laughter. The stage manager came on with a handkerchief and helped me to gather it up. I thought he was going to keep it. This thought was conveyed to the audience and increased their laughter, especially when he walked off with it with me anxiously following him. Not until he handed it to Mother did I return and continue to sing. I was quite at home."[12]

Charlie was a natural entertainer. At home, he often used to put up an act and sing and dance along to amuse his mother and brother. This interest in theatre was instilled into him by his mother, who often encouraged him to perform in front of others as well.

Once during a recess in school, he was reciting *Miss Priscilla's Cat* to one of his friends and a teacher, who was passing by, saw his performance and got amused. "I was brought before every classroom in the school, both boys and girls, and made to recite it."[13] It was a comedy recitation which his mother had seen on a window of a newspaper stand. She found it to be funny and had copied it out to show it to her boys.

After Charlie had spent his time in his father's house and much after his mother's return from the Cane Hill asylum, he got a job which somewhat was the beginning of his career and dreams. He found a place in a troupe of dancers by the name of Eight Lancashire Lads. This arrangement was done by Charlie's father, who knew Mr. Jackson, the manager of the troupe.

Mr. Jackson was a middle-aged school teacher and all his children too were a part of the troupe. Charlie's mother Hannah was a bit sceptical at first about letting her son be away from her but as soon as she met Mr. Jackson, she was assured that he was in safe hands.

Charlie was not a little boy anymore and, as a result, he wasn't comfortable with people staring at him while he performed. It was only natural that he had stage fright for his first few performances. He also started having dreams of a career on stage. "I would have liked to be a boy comedian – but that would have required nerve, to stand on the stage alone. Nevertheless, my first impulse to do something other than dance was to be funny. My idea was a double act, two boys dressed as comedy tramps. I told it to one of the other boys and we decided to become partners. It became our cherished dream. We would call ourselves 'Bristol and Chaplin, the Millionaire Tramps', and would wear tramp whiskers and big diamond rings. It embraced every aspect of what we thought would be funny and profitable, but, alas, it never materialised."[14]

This proves that Charlie had always dreamt of becoming a gentlemanly tramp, a character which was introduced by him and is his trademark. The phrase 'Millionaire Tramps' contradicts itself in every aspect and yet, Charlie could think of such a bizarre character at such a tender age. It is something to be amazed at.

Eight Lancashire Lads toured various provinces all over the country and wherever they went, there was a combination of vaudeville and circus. As a result, Charlie got to learn many new things, including acrobats and, in the process, he also came in contact with a variety of clowns. One such clown that he learnt a great deal from was Marceline.

"Marceline's comedy was droll and charming and London went wild over him.... Years later Marceline went to the New York Hippodrome, where he was also a sensation. But when the Hippodrome abolished the circus ring, Marceline was soon forgotten. In 1918, or thereabouts, Ringing Brothers' three-ring circus came to Los Angeles and Marceline was with them. I expected that he would be featured, but I was shocked to find him just one of many clowns that ran around the enormous ring – a great artist lost in the vulgar extravagance of a three-ring circus.... A year later, in New York, he committed suicide."[15]

And then there was the comedy juggler, Zarmo. Charlie was really amazed by his acts. Zarmo was not too popular on stage but his dedication towards his skills and his hours of relentless practice was something that Charlie appreciated.

Charlie also admired various other such comedians.

Bransby Williams was an actor who imitated various fascinating characters from literature which generated Charlie's interest in the subject. Mr. Williams was particularly fond of the characters from the books of Charles Dickens. Often Charlie imitated Mr. Williams's imitation of the old man from *The Old Curiosity Shop* (Charles Dickens) and was once seen by Mr. Jackson while he was doing so. Mr. Jackson was so impressed by his performance that he asked Charlie to put that act in their next show.

But when Charlie did so at a theatre in Middlesbrough, it was not received well by the audience. The problem was not with the act but with the voice. Charlie was so engrossed in his character that he did not realise that he should have spoken louder as the audience could not hear him. As a result, no one enjoyed his performance, which disappointed him much.

Once when the troupe was in London, Charlie came to meet his mother. She looked at him and got worried about his health. She wrote a letter to Mr. Jackson about it, who, in turn, thought that he could not keep Charlie in his troupe if his mother cannot bear their separation. And hence, Charlie had to leave the troupe.

As soon as he left, he developed asthma, which terrified his mother because she had been suspecting that something was wrong with him during the time he was with Eight Lancashire Lads. Now her fear had turned into reality but when she showed him to the doctors, they said he would be fine after a while.

Charlie recalls that Sydney during this time had probably been living with his grandfather, Hannah's father. So it was just Charlie that Hannah had to worry about. Thus, they both kept moving from place to place until finally they took a small loft at 3, Pownall Terrace.

It was around this time that Charlie tasted luxury. His mother met an old friend who had become rich by marrying a wealthy colonel. The friend invited her and Charlie to her house in Stockwell to come and live with them for a few weeks.

Charlie really had a time of his life, as they were the guests to a wealthy family where he was being tended to by servants and was given proper food. Even his asthma was treated while he was there, when one of the residents suggested him a cure.

Back home, Charlie missed the luxury but also realised that he needed to find a proper job, now that he desired to lead a better life. He was not even twelve yet and had already gained a sense of responsibility that he bore to himself and his mother.

Meanwhile, Sydney, who was fourteen now, left school and found a job. He started living with them again and helped the family. Their mother held her stitching job while Charlie had nothing else to do. He was becoming increasingly embarrassed by their state of affairs, especially when his friends looked at his torn and patched clothes and mocked him with their eyes.

Charlie's father died during this stage of their life. He was only thirty-seven and had developed cirrhosis, which was due to his alcoholism. He was buried by his younger brother, whom Charlie calls Uncle Albert in the autobiography.

It was time for Charlie to now be serious about working. He had decided that he wanted to earn money for a business that he wished to start. Hannah had completely ignored his pestering about giving him money, but later agreed to let him leave school and look for a job. He was only twelve years old.

His first job was at a chandler's shop, which supplied household items such as soap, oil, candles and sweets. He helped the owner with various chores, and, in the meantime, munched on the sweets and biscuit supplies. This made him sick and eventually he left the job.

Then he joined the office of Dr. Kinsey Taylor as a receptionist. He loved to entertain the patients while they waited for their appointment but when it came to cleaning the windows and floors, he hated his job.

Soon after, Dr. Taylor married a rich lady and they took Charlie as their page-boy. This meant that Charlie had to live in their house, which he enjoyed too much. He lost this job when he was caught blowing an eight-foot long iron-pipe which was supposed to be a showpiece and not to be played with.

Next, he worked with W.H. Smith and Son, who were newsagents and publishers. He had to leave the job when the owner found out that he was underage. He also worked as a glassblower for a day which he had initially thought to be a romantic idea.

Then he worked at Straker's, who were printers. They had a Wharfedale printing machine which was about twenty feet in size. Charlie told them that he could run it. But when he saw the machine, he did not know what to do. "He showed me the lever, then put the beast at half speed. It started to roll, grind and grunt; I thought it was going to devour me. The sheets were enormous; you could have wrapped me in one.... The first day I was a nervous wreck from the hungry brute wanting to get ahead of me. Nevertheless, I was given the job at twelve shillings per week."[16]

Charlie enjoyed this job for three weeks after which he suffered from Influenza. In the meantime, Sydney found a proper job as a bugler on a Donovan and Castle Line passenger boat. After his first trip, he returned home for a month and brought with him some extra money with which the trio enjoyed a lot, buying ice-cream and other such delicacies.

Charlie was capable of generating new business ideas. Once he asked his mother to give him all the old clothes. With that he went to the market, trying to sell them off. Although it wasn't a success, Charlie still did not stop trying.

Then he started working a pair of travelling toy makers, who had come all the way from Glasgow. Charlie learnt their art and when they were gone, he tried continuing that business alone. But when he realised that their room was getting too crowded with his mother's sewing and his toy making, he gave up his work as it hardly gave him enough money.

Events before Hannah's Return to the Asylum

Charlie knew more of his grandfather than he ever knew his father. His grandfather lived nearby and was a cobbler by profession. He did well for himself and often helped out her daughter in taking care of his grandchildren. But since the past few months, he was not well. He was not able to work as his hands were swollen and, therefore, he got admitted into an infirmary.

Whenever Hannah visited him, she brought with him a bag full of eggs. At first, Charlie did not know how or from where these eggs were coming, until he started going to the infirmary himself. "When his rheumatism allowed him, he worked in the kitchen, whence came our eggs. On visiting days, he was usually in bed, and from his bedside cabinet would surreptitiously hand me a large bag of them, which I quickly stowed in my sailor's tunic before departing."[17]

After a few weeks of stay, his grandfather was cured and discharged, which brought with it the end of the egg days.

This time, Sydney was out for long. He had not returned even after seven weeks at sea. This worried their mother and she wrote to his office. They replied by saying that her son was sick and was getting treatment. Hannah was worried again and this affected her health to a great extent.

When another week went by and Sydney was not home, Charlie started worrying a bit about his mother. But certainly he did not comprehend what was about to happen. For hours she used to sit by the window watching outside and doing nothing else. She became numb to all feelings, hardly smiling or reacting to anything around her. This failed to come to the notice of Charlie.

During this time, Hannah's friend from theatre, Mrs. McCarthy came to live nearby. They were well off and lived in the Walcott Mansion. Charlie often went to play with her son Wally and sometimes even stayed for dinner. Hannah rarely visited them and Mrs. McCarthy frequently asked Charlie about her health.

Hannah was not well. She was suffering from malnutrition. If only Charlie knew this, he could have taken care of her in time.

One day while coming back home from McCarthy's place, Charlie found a bunch of children, who told him that his mother had gone insane. Apparently, she had been knocking at all the neighbour's doors asking for Sydney. She later complained to Charlie saying she suspected that someone was keeping him away from her.

Charlie could not understand why her mother thought this way. He even blamed himself for not foreseeing this. When the doctor came to see her, he declared her as insane and ordered her to go to the infirmary. He also informed Charlie that she was undernourished and that she would be properly taken care of under the constant watch of the nurses.

Charlie left her in the infirmary which was one mile away from home. "As I walked from the hospital towards home, I could feel only a numbing sadness. Yet I was relieved, for I knew that Mother would be better off in the hospital than sitting alone in that dark room with nothing to eat. But that heart-breaking look as they led her away, I shall never forget."[18]

Charlie was torn between relief and sadness. He did not know whether this decision was the right one. On one side, he thought that his mother would be taken care of, but on the other, she would be living all alone. The thought of leaving her alone in the hospital saddened him the most.

When he got back home, his heart filled with an emptiness seeing the vacant room. There was nothing to eat except a candy which his mother had offered to him in the morning. Charlie curled up and cried. There was a limit to what a twelve-year-old child could bear.

Next day, Charlie got word that his mother was transferred to Cane Hill Asylum, which was around twenty miles from home. He decided that he would go to visit her after Sydney came back.

Now that he was alone, he survived on whatever food he could find anywhere and tried to stay out of the room as much as possible. He even stopped visiting McCarthy's house as he did not want them to know about his mother.

Wandering about here and there, he tried to find a job. Soon he came across a group of woodcutters who lived in a shed at night and worked hard during the day. Charlie somehow managed to join them. He was more interested in the labour work of cutting the woods than in its sale. He worked with them for quite a while and, as time passed, he made friends with them.

Once their boss took them to a theatre in which Fred Karno's comedy show was being presented for that week. Charlie naturally was excited because he aspired to be a comedian some day.

He continued working with them until Sydney's return. When Charlie went to receive him at the station, he broke the news of their mother's illness which saddened Sydney too much. He had brought with him some good money and other items for them to be able to live a better life, but their mother wasn't there now to share it with them. "The same day Sydney went shopping and outfitted me with new clothes, and that night, all dressed up, we sat in the stalls of the South London Music Hall. During the performance Sydney kept repeating: 'Just think what tonight would have meant to Mother.'"[19]

A few days later, they went to meet their mother and were upset to see her in such pathetic condition. The doctor told them that she had not yet recovered from malnutrition and that she needed proper medical care.

❑

Change in Fortune

Charlie often went to Blackmore Theatrical Agency looking for an acting job. Once he was lingering around till the end and was seen by an official there. The man asked him whether he had registered himself and when Charlie replied in negative, he was taken to another room and his name and other details were taken down.

A few days later, Charlie received a postcard, asking him to be present at the theatre for a job. He was getting the part of Billie, the page-boy, in *Sherlock Holmes*. For a period of forty weeks, Charlie was set now. He had never held a job for so long.

Meanwhile, he was also asked to play another part for another play, *Jim, the Romance of a Cockney*, which was for a shorter duration. Charlie was a sharp boy. He instantly told them that he would consult his brother about it. This incident itself proves his professionalism. He was a nonentity then, yet that didn't come in the way of his handling of matters. And Sydney was one step ahead of Charlie. He told him that he deserved a better salary than what was being offered to him and that they should go and negotiate.

Although they did not win, a hint of Sydney's future role in Charlie's life was beginning to show. He helped

Charlie in every way possible, even in making him memorise his part. Although the play wasn't that successful, Charlie received a few praises, wherein he was commended for his comic role.

Then the tour for *Sherlock Holmes* began. Charlie was to live with a couple, who were employees of the company, but neither Charlie nor the couple liked each other much. Hence, Charlie, ended up living alone throughout the tour. Sometimes, he managed to stay in the landlady's house whenever they offered him a place, but otherwise, he was on his own.

Meanwhile, in his autobiography, Charlie talks about his brother's letters which he used to receive quite regularly, but to which he never replied. He recalls one particular letter in which Sydney talked about their struggles and the bond which they had established as brothers since their mother's illness. This moved Charlie so much that he instantly replied to his letter and, since then, they managed to maintain that bond all their lives.

Soon the forty weeks were over but the tour extended for another eight weeks, playing in the suburbs of London. After this, *Sherlock Holmes* was to have a second tour for which Charlie was asked to stay. Charlie also managed to talk to the Company about giving Sydney a small part in the play. Both the brothers were now a part of the tour. During this time, they left their Pownall Terrace room and took a better place.

As soon as their second tour was over, their mother returned home. According to the doctors of Cane Hill, she was much better now and, therefore, they asked Sydney to take her back. But to Charlie, she was not the same anymore. She had become detached and unemotional. She smiled less often and did not seem excited about anything.

Charlie and Sydney tried taking her with them for their next tour. She felt happy for a while when she tried helping them with cooking food for the members, but after a few weeks, she wanted to return home.

A few months in her rented apartment, and Hannah was sick again. The cause of her illness was not known this time, as anyone could see financially they were better off and she did not even have to worry about her children as they were doing quite well. Hence, she was again sent back to Cane Hill Asylum.

Both the brothers were on tour and, therefore, could not meet their mother at once.

After some time, the rights of *Sherlock Holmes* were bought by another company and they toured in smaller towns with lesser salaries.

Soon Charlie was offered to play the role of Billie in *The Painful Predicament of Sherlock Holmes* which was directed by William Gillette. He left his current job and joined Mr. Gillette in London.

He was now sixteen. It had been more than three years since he had joined theatre and he was enjoying every bit of it. He met new people, and they did not instantly love him, but his work was always appreciated.

At the end of the tour of *Holmes*, Charlie was asked to meet with Mr. and Mrs. Kendal for a new job. When Charlie met Mrs. Kendal, she asked him to come again the next day for reading a part in a new play. They were going to tour the provinces. Charlie refused to work with them because he wanted to stay in London. "'I am sorry, madam,' I replied coldly, 'but I cannot accept anything out of town.' And with that I raised my hat, walked out of the foyer, hailed a passing cab – and was out of work for ten months."[20]

Sydney's tour had also ended by this time, but unlike Charlie, he found another job. He joined the comedy troupe of Charlie Manon. While Sydney was working for them, Fred Karno noticed his work and hired him. Fred Karno's theatrical enterprise was considered the best among all at that time. Thus, began the good luck for one of the brothers.

Charlie was beginning to become less serious about anything in life. He had reached that stage where nothing seemed of any importance. All he wanted was attention. As is evident from these lines from the autobiography, "The theatre meant a livelihood and nothing more. Through this haze and confusion I lived alone...,. I really wanted romance and adventure."[21]

He later found some work at Casey's Circus. He was the leading man in the show and it helped him develop as a comedian. He lived with Mrs. Fields and her daughters as a paying guest and stayed with them for a while, even after leaving the circus. He became unemployed again, while Sydney had become one of the stars of Fred Karno. "He was now a leading comedian with Fred Karno, and had often spoken to Karno about his talented young brother, but Karno turned a deaf ear, because he thought I was too young."[22]

Then something happened that depressed Charlie for a while. He had prepared a comic act which was to be presented on a week's trial in Forester's Music Hall.

What happened can be best described in Charlie's own words, "After the first couple of jokes, the audience started throwing coins and orange-peel and stamping their feet and booing...I began to hurry and talk faster as the jeers, the raspberries, and the throwing of coins and orange-peel increased. When I came off the stage, I did not wait to hear the verdict from the management; I went straight to the dressing room, took off my make-up, left the theatre and never returned, not even to collect my music books.... I did my best to erase that night's horror from my mind, but it left an indelible mark on my confidence. That ghastly experience taught me to see myself in a truer light; I realized I was not a vaudeville comedian, I had not that intimate, come-hither faculty with an audience; and I consoled myself with being a character comedian."[23]

This incident also reminds one about a similar experience that Charlie's mother went through. She had been laughed at on stage when she lost her voice and it was rather embarrassing. Charlie had not understood what was happening then, but now he clearly grasped the situation and was found to be deeply disheartened by it.

Charlie then got a week's job to play the lead in a play, which did not do much good to his confidence.

Charlie also tried his hand at scripting. He wrote a play *Twelve Just Men* which was a slapstick comedy, involving a panel of jury arguing a case where a promise was broken. It was accepted by Charcoate, a vaudeville hypnotist, who gave Charlie the money to direct the play. Charlie had started with the rehearsals but three days later, the producer cancelled his show.

At a time when it seemed that Charlie's luck had ran out on him, he found a chance which changed his life forever. *Sherlock Holmes* had only played a small part, but this opportunity was a complete climax to the first 'Act' of his life.

Apparently, Sydney had been successful in bringing his brother to the notice of Fred Karno and now Karno wanted to meet Charlie for a part in his show. He offered him to play opposite Harry Weldon, a successful comedian, in *The Football Match*. Charlie was only too obliged to accept it.

"On the opening night at the Coliseum, my nerves were wound tight like a clock. That night meant re-establishing my confidence and wiping out the disgrace of that nightmare at the Foresters'... The moment I walked on to stage I was relieved, everything was clear. I entered with my back to the audience – an idea of my own. From the back I looked immaculate, dressed in a frock-coat, top hat, cane and spats – a typical Edwardian villain. Then I turned, showing my red nose. There was a laugh. That ingratiated me with the audience. I shrugged melodramatically, then snapped my fingers and veered across the stage, tripping over a dumb-bell. Then my cane became entangled with an upright punching bag, which rebounded and slapped me in the face. I swaggered and swung, hitting myself with my cane on the side of the head. The audience roared."[24]

This was how Charlie's dream came true. He had now become a complete actor, and was no longer called a child artist. After the first few nights, he signed a one-year contract with Mr. Karno.

It was now time for the brothers to have a new house. They took a flat in Brixton Road and furnished it with proper furniture, crowding it with all they had ever dreamt of. Charlie and Sydney had started earning so much that they even decided to support their grandfather, who wasn't in good health since his last visit to the infirmary. Visits to their mother often saddened them and, thus, they limited those calls and tried to concentrate more on their work.

Charlie was to go through another change in his life. Fred Karno was a man who did not just limit his tours to London and other provinces. He also took his group to far off countries and Charlie soon experienced the touch and romance of France.

It was only a month long tour but Charlie was excited. He had never been out of England and France was some place that he had always wanted to go. In the autobiography, he talks about his father being half French.

Charlie met new people and fell in love with the country. One of Sydney's cousins, who lived there, acted as his guide, helping him visit the best of Paris. They gave successful shows all over the city and Karno was happy with Charlie's performances.

When they returned to England, Charlie was given the role of Harry Weldon for the next tour of *The Football Match.* This was a big achievement for him, as he was going to play the lead in one of the best shows of Karno and that too at Oxford Music Hall, which was one of the best theatres in England.

But right before the show's rehearsals, he was diagnosed with laryngitis and, hence, could not speak for a long time. This saddened Charlie a lot but he was helpless. Although he still played the part, the audience kept complaining about not being able to hear him. Karno was much disappointed and put him back to *Mumming Birds*.

It was now time for Charlie's contract to end and, thus, he wanted a raise. After the Oxford incident, it was unlikely that Charlie was even going to be with Karno's company any more. Karno complained that people were talking about Charlie being an incompetent actor. But Charlie was not a man who could take such comments without being affected. He confronted Karno asking him if he too thought that Charlie was not a good actor.

At the end of one year, Charlie signed a new contract and, surprisingly, even received a raise.

❑

Off to America

"When in 1910 Charlie Chaplin signed a contract with the Fred Karno Comedy Company under which he engaged himself to play as leading comedian for a long tour of the United States and Canada, he took a step which indirectly had an important bearing on his future. He had worked, as we have seen, for a considerable time with the Fred Karno organization, and Alfred Reeves, the manager of the particular company, with which he was associated, was a close personal friend."[25]

Alfred Reeves had come to England in search for a comedian, whom he wanted to take with him to America. Charlie was lucky as he was playing the leading role in *Skating* and his work caught Reeves's attention. Reeves made friends with Charlie and told Karno that he had found the man he was looking for.

When Charlie decided to go to America, he also decided to leave London forever. Although his tour was for a particular time period, he had all plans to settle there and look for another job. And, thus, he bade good-bye to England, without even once meeting his mother or his brother for the last time. To cover that, he only wrote one short letter to Sydney saying that he was going to America and that he would keep in touch.

Charlie did come back to England after the tour was over, but it was for a short duration.

The troupe went to America via Canada. They first landed in Toronto, which Charlie found as promising. But when he reached New York, the corporate world seemed quite gloomy at first and he was a little disappointed.

"We had left England in the middle of a bitter cold September and arrived in New York in an Indian summer with a temperature of eighty degrees; and as I walked along Broadway, it began to light up with myriads of coloured electric bulbs and sparkled like a brilliant jewel. And in the warm night, my attitude changed and the meaning of America came to me: the tall skyscrapers, the brilliant, gay lights, the thrilling display of advertisements stirred me with hope and a sense of adventure. 'That is it!' I said to myself. 'This is where I belong to!'"[26]

Charlie's first act was not well received and, as Charlie points out, it was not made for the American audience. Nonetheless, they had to perform the same act for the rest of the week which did not get them good reviews.

Charlie felt humiliated and dejected and was thankful that he did not have anyone to share this feeling with. But soon he got over it and started thinking about pursuing another job. He admitted that he was not yet dedicated to his art.

Since their show was not going too well, they had decided to pack their bags and leave for England at once. But then they got to perform at the Fifth Avenue Theatre, which mostly consisted of an English audience. They got such good response there that it helped them to stay in America for some more time.

The troupe toured all over America and then came back to New York, where Charlie performed in the memorable *A Night in an English Music Hall.* Mack Sennett, who had later formed the Keystone Film Company, was there on one of the nights and was impressed by Charlie's performance as the drunken old man.

David Robinson, who wrote a biography on Charlie Chaplin, describes this particular act in these words, "The sketch opens with fortissimo music as a girl shows an elderly gentleman and his nephew – an objectionable boy, armed with peashooter, tin trumpet, and picnic hamper – into the lower O.P. box. The Inebriated Swell is settled into the prompt side box, and instantly embarks upon some business of a very Chaplinesque character. He peels the glove from his right hand, tips the waiting attendant, and then, forgetting that he has already removed his glove, absently attempts to peel it off again. He tries to light his cigar from the electric light beside the box. The boy holds out a match for him, and in gracefully inclining to reach it, the Swell falls out of the box."[27]

Now it was time for the tour to come to an end and for them to go back to England. Charlie was not happy. He roamed about in the streets admiring the beauty of America, not wanting to leave at all. Such was his determination that once he had even formed an alliance with a Texan trapeze performer, deciding to become partners in a business of raising pigs, which eventually they had to give up.

It was Charlie's immature tenacity to stay in America for which he was ready to do anything. But when nothing worked out, he came back to England after a few successful shows with the sole purpose of returning to America.

Upon reaching home, Charlie found out that his flat was gone and that Sydney was now married. He had come back after a couple of years, so it was natural that there would have been a few changes, but these he had never expected.

During this time, Charlie and Sydney also decided to shift their mother to a private institution since she was not doing well in the current one and also because they could now afford the expenses involved.

Charlie was back to work and toured around England for a few weeks, after which Karno announced that they were going back to America for their second tour. Charlie was obviously thrilled and swore that he would never come back now. This time he even met Sydney before leaving.

In America, Karno's group performed all over the country and had a very hectic schedule. Charlie was so exhausted that he needed some time off; so he went to New York and spent a night at a luxurious hotel room.

"Now I would go to New York and shed myself of tenth-rate vaudeville and its whole drab existence.... I took a room at the Astor Hotel, which was quite grandiose in those days.... The room cost $4.50 a day.... Passing through the lobby with all its gilt and plush did something to me emotionally, so that when I reached my room, I felt I wanted to weep."[28]

Keystone's Offer to Charlie

After joining the troupe back in Philadelphia, Charlie read a telegram addressed to Mr. Reeves, which contained a piece of news that Charlie had never dreamt of. It was from Mr. Kessel, whom Charlie first mistook to be a lawyer. It turned out that Mr. Kessel was associated with Keystone Film Company, which was formed by Mr. Mack Sennett, and that they wanted to hire Charlie as an actor for motion pictures.

Charlie was offered double the salary of what he was getting at Karno's Company, yet he tried negotiating for a bit more. They eventually found a middle path to which both parties agreed and Charlie decided to join them as soon as his contract with Karno was over.

❑

A Parallel Universe

"I remember an evening in our one room in the basement at Oakley Street. I lay in bed recovering from a fever. Sydney had gone out to night school and Mother and I were alone. It was late afternoon, and she sat with her back to the window reading, acting and explaining in her inimitable way the New Testament and Christ's love and pity for the poor and for little children. Perhaps her emotion was due to my illness, but she gave the most luminous and appealing interpretation of Christ that I have ever heard of or seen. She spoke of his tolerant understanding; of the woman who had sinned and was to be stoned by the mob, and of his words to them: 'He that is without sin among you, let him first cast a stone at her.'

She read into the dusk, stopping only to light the lamp, then told of the faith that Jesus inspired in the sick, that they had only to touch the hem of his garment to be healed.

She told of the hate and jealousy of the High Priests and Pharisees, and described Jesus and his arrest and his calm dignity before Pontius Pilate, who, washing his hands, said (this she acted out histrionically): 'I find no fault with this man.' She told how they stripped and scourged him and, placing a crown of thorns on his head, mocked and spat at him, saying: 'Hail, King of Jews!'

As she continued, tears welled up in her eyes. She told of Simon helping to carry Christ's cross and the appealing look of gratitude Jesus gave him; she told of the repentant thief, dying with him on a cross and asking for forgiveness, and of Jesus saying: 'Today shalt thou be with me in Paradise.' And from the cross looking down at his mother, saying: 'Woman, behold thy son.' And in his last dying agony crying out: 'My God, why hast thou forsaken me?' And we both wept.

'Don't you see,' said Mother, 'how human he was; like all of us, he too suffered doubt.'

Mother had so carried me away that I wanted to die that very night and meet Jesus. But Mother was not so enthusiastic. 'Jesus wants you to live first and fulfil your destiny here,' she said. In that dark room in the basement at Oakley Street, Mother illuminated to me the kindliest light this world has ever known, which has endowed literature and the theatre with their greatest and richest themes: love, pity and humanity."[29]

Charlie must have been really young when this night happened, but this dramatic description of the same in his autobiography also tells another story.

When Charlie was in America for the second time, he was trying various ways and means by which he could stay back, as he did not want to see England again. One of his schemes was to try and educate himself. He was of the opinion that, by studying, he would be able to get a better job. So he bought second hand books in an attempt to be able to not stay ignorant. "I wanted to know, not for the love of knowledge but as a defence against the world's contempt for the ignorant."[30]

The books which he read inspired him a bit, reassuring his beliefs on religion. Charlie was not exactly religious, despite the fact that his childhood was filled with stories of Jesus. Yet, it did affect him in some way.

One of Charlie's sons wrote in his book, "Dad was vague about who it was to whom he addressed his prayer. I never heard him speak of God as a personal power or conjecture about what comes after death. He never even mentioned death as far as I can recall. He wasn't one to adopt an organized religion, and he didn't care for ritualistic services, though he openly and ardently admired the architecture of churches and synagogues. He never forced his own beliefs on Syd and me, though occasionally he would speak of them to us.

'I'm not an atheist,' I can remember him saying on more than one occasion. 'I'm definitely an agnostic. Some scientists say that if the world were to stop revolving we'd all disintegrate. But the world keeps on going. Something must be holding us all in place – some Supreme Force. But what it is I couldn't tell you.'"[31]

Charlie was like any other normal human being. Given that he had a rough childhood, living in poverty with a single mother who couldn't hold herself, he turned out just fine. In fact, he did more than just fine for himself.

He lived his teenage years most interestingly. He used to get into drunken brawls, visit brothels and spend as much as he could afford. But in doing all that, he always had a sense of responsibility towards himself.

Charlie's romantic episodes are even more interesting to read. He first felt the presence of a woman when he was sixteen. Marie Doro had come to London with Mr. Gillette, who had played the lead in *The Painful Predicament of Sherlock Holmes*, in which Charlie played Billie.

About her Charlie said, "She was so devastatingly beautiful that I resented her....I had just turned sixteen, and the propinquity of this sudden radiance evoked my determination not to be obsessed by it. But, oh God, she was beautiful! It was love at first sight."[32]

Charlie once also fancied Phoebe, the youngest daughter of Mrs. Fields, when he was living with them as their paying guest in London. His work with Mr. Gillette was over and he was then with Casey's Circus.

Hetty Kelly was Charlie's actual first love. He had met her during one of his shows for Karno's Company in Streatham. She was a part of a song-and-dance group known by the name of Bert Coutts' Yankee-Doodle Girls. At that time, Charlie was almost nineteen.

He managed to ask Hetty to go on a date with him and to his surprise, she even agreed. He had a thing about beauty. She had only appeared in front of him in make-up and costume before; so on the day they were supposed to meet for a date, Charlie dreaded what she would look like when she came up in front of him in her normal attire. But Charlie did not regret it. She looked absolutely amazing and he almost fell in love with her, although she did not reciprocate those feelings yet, at least not on their first meeting. "How little she understood what it all meant to me. It had little to do with sex; more important was her association. To meet elegance and beauty in my station of life was rare."[33]

They met several times after that. Hetty was only fifteen years old, so it was natural that she might suddenly feel nervous about the whole affair, and so she did. She told him that she could not see him anymore because she was too young.

And thus, Charlie felt his first heart-break.

The way Charlie describes it, the episode was quite dramatic. He had confronted her about whether she loved him or not and for a fifteen-year-old, it's too early to even think about commitments. Hence, they broke up.

Charlie went to see her again the next day but nothing happened.

After this, Charlie never really fell in love with another girl until he was about fifty. That was when he got married for the last time. In between, he fancied several girls, had numerous affairs, and four marriages.

Charlie was a man of his own accord. He never listened to anybody, rarely followed any rules and since he had no one to look after him during his tours, he did what he wanted. Once he kept a rabbit in his room, against the wishes of the landlady. He even trained it to hide in a box every time someone came up to his room, until someone caught him and took it away.

When Charlie was in America, he also watched opera one night. It was in German and he could not understand a word, yet he could feel all the emotions and, suddenly, a drop of tear flowed down. He could not comprehend the exact reason behind it. He wrote in his autobiography, "It seemed to sum up all the travail of my life. I could hardly control myself; what people next to me must have thought I don't know, but I came away limp and emotionally shattered."[34]

It's the little experiences which one goes through in life that makes a person complete. Charlie was someone who was moulded by his loving mother, his doting brother and a father he never had. Had his childhood been any different, probably we would never have seen the *Tramp*.

Enters Film Industry

There was a time when Cinema actually meant something much more than just entertainment despite the fact that they were produced just for entertainment. And it was during that time that Charlie Chaplin made films.

Charlie's most famous character which has been portrayed in many of his movies is him in the role of a 'Tramp'. Many argue about the first movie in which he appeared as that character. It's not that he has played the same character in every movie, but only that this particular character caught everyone's fancy and it is what Charlie is most remembered for.

John Kimber, in his book, *The Art of Charlie Chaplin*, talked about the controversy regarding Charlie's first appearance as the 'Tramp'. "*Kid Auto Races at Venice* was possibly not, as has often been supposed, the first film in which Chaplin wore his famous costume. There is a conflict of testimony on this point between Chaplin and his biographers, but it was certainly the first such film to be released (in February 1914), so there is some justification for regarding it as particularly significant. The temptation to do so is anyway almost irresistible. *Kid Auto Races* would not merit much attention but for the value bestowed upon it by hindsight."[35]

So what was this costume which made Charlie famous overnight? After a short appearance in his first movie, Mr. Sennet asked Charlie to put on a funny make-up. What followed has been put well in words by Charlie himself. "I had no idea what make-up to put on. I did not like my get-up as the press reporter in *Making a Living*. However, on the way to the wardrobe, I thought I would dress in baggy pants, big shoes, a cane, and a derby hat. I wanted everything to be a contradiction: the pants baggy, the coat tight, the hat small and the shoes large. I was undecided whether to look old or young, but remembering Sennett had expected me to be a much older man, I added a small moustache, which, I reasoned, would add age without hiding my expression. I had no idea of the character. But the moment I was dressed, the clothes and the make-up made me feel the person he was. I began to know him, and by the time I walked on to the stage, he was fully born. When I confronted Sennett, I assumed the character and strutted about, swinging my cane and parading before him."[36]

And from where did he get that walk? David Robinson wrote in one of his articles, "The Tramp himself is a figure from Victorian London – Chaplin recalled that he had based the characteristic walk on the gait of a rheumaticky old man called Rummy Binks, who took care of the horses at the Queen's Head in Black Prince Road (then Broad Street), Kennington."[37]

The first scene which Charlie did as the 'Tramp' involved him stumbling on to people and raising his hat and apologising. It was an improvising scene in which he kept thinking on the spot and doing whatever he thought could look funny. As soon as Charlie started his act in front of the camera, everyone on the set stopped what they were doing and watched him. There was a whole crowd who was enjoying his performance. Never before had such a thing happened on the sets of Mr. Sennett, and Charlie was exhilarated.

After a few films, Sennett started having problems with the way Charlie worked. Mr. Lehrman was one of the good directors who worked for Sennett and Charlie often tried to advise him about a few shots. This may have irked Lehrman and when Sennett himself was directing Charlie, he realised the same thing.

At first Sennett was patient, even accepting some tips which Charlie gave but, later on, after an incident on the set, he told him straight to either follow the instructions or leave. This happened when Charlie was working under the direction of Miss Mabel Normand.

It was her first film and Charlie did not trust her with the job. Miss Normand was not even attempting to listen to any of Charlie's suggestions which ultimately led to him walking out of the set. When Sennett got to know about it, he confronted Charlie.

"'You'll do what you're told or get out, contract or no contract,' he said.

I was very calm. 'Mr. Sennett,' I answered, 'I earned my bread and cheese before I came here, and if I'm fired – well, I'm fired. But I'm conscientious and just as keen to make a good picture as you are.'"[38]

Next day, Charlie was back to work and Sennett was surprisingly very affectionate towards him. It was much later that Charlie got to know about the real reason behind this change in attitude. Sennett had found out that Charlie was becoming quite popular among the audience and that there was a great demand for his movies.

Now Charlie was even more confident about his position in the company. He wished to direct movies and Sennett let him. He wanted to write stories, and Sennett let him. Charlie's first movie as a Director was *Caught in the Rain.*

When Charlie was a kid and used to visit the McCarthys, he often played with their son Wally. They used to make up stories and act them out and Charlie always directed Wally, telling him what to do. So when Charlie assumed the role of a Director, it was as if he was born to do it.

Charlie also taught the company the art of pantomime. They initially tried to argue that theatre tactics had little to do with the techniques involved in film making but, eventually, they were grateful to learn from him.

Charlie had learnt how to mime very early in his life. He had performed in various events in his school days and also later when he started working in the theatre. It came naturally to him, and Keystone at that time had little idea about the greatness of their teacher.

Films with Keystone

Charlie made over thirty films with Keystone Film Company, a number of which he directed himself. Some of the popular ones are *His Prehistoric Past, Caught in the Rain, Mabel's Strange Predicament, Laffing Gas, The Knockout, Dough and Dynamite, The New Janitor* and so on.

Theatre was surely different from films and Charlie had begun to see the difference. He started liking the movie making business mainly because he thought that it liberated him. He had the freedom to choose his own plots, his own style and story. There was no rigidity, and there was absolutely no fixed technique. He did not even have to repeat the same performance day after day. In fact, most of his films were completed within three days of shooting and then he could think of the next one.

Caught in the Rain, which was released on May 4, 1914, was about a love triangle in which Charlie pursues a married lady. The main gag in the film is when Charlie tries to climb stairs and repeatedly falls.

Laffing Gas (or *Laughing Gas*, July 9, 1914) was one of Keystone's best comedy movie ever produced. It had Charlie playing an ill-mannered assistant of a dentist, who abused the other employees and the patients sitting in the waiting room. Charlie also tries to act as the dentist in the latter's absence and takes advantage of a lady patient.

"....In the same film, the extraction pincers are employed to secure pretty girl-patient by the nose so that Charlie can kiss her – it is their grasping properties that inspire him here, and the gag is also a good example of Charlie's shrewd eye for any kind of erotic advantage."[39]

Previously, Keystone Company was all about chases and gags and improvising stories on the spot. Charlie brought with him a decent story running chronologically, which did not always involve chasing as the only source of laughter. It was slapstick yes, but it had more than what the other movies had provided before.

Charlie was getting along well with both Miss Mabel Normand and Sennett. They had become good friends, almost always having dinner together. It was during this time that Charlie met Peggy Pierce. She was Charlie's first romantic affair, if spending four days with Hetty Kelly doesn't count. He was mad about her, and she was the reason he came to work with a smile on his face every morning. But this romance did not last long and, as Charlie described it, it was a 'lost cause'.

After having directed several movies, Charlie suggested Sennett to take Sydney into his company. Sennett was only too happy to agree as he liked Charlie a lot. Sydney had yet to make a mark in the film industry and, as history has it, he became quite a successful actor on his own.

When Sydney arrived, he was so excited to see Charlie that he kept talking about how his movies were doing really well in England. He was extremely proud of his little brother and told him that, back home, whenever he told anyone that he was Charlie's brother, their behaviour used to suddenly change and that they used to begin treating him respectfully.

It was the time of the First World War and since America wasn't much affected by it, their film industry too did well. At such times, in fact, people needed to watch more comedies. Charlie, at this point in time, wasn't much into theme-based movies. The time for that came when he made *The Great Dictator* (1940), a movie hinting toward Adolf Hitler's reign in Germany during the Second World War.

Charlie's contract was about to end and since he had become quite successful, naturally his demands were becoming quite exorbitant. He now demanded almost ten times his previous salary but Sennett wasn't ready to agree to his terms. As much as he wanted Charlie to stay, he knew that he could not afford him now.

Charlie in his mind had already decided to leave if he did not get what he demanded. He even asked Sydney whether he would join him if he chose to start his own company, but Sydney refused.

Meanwhile, Charlie started getting offers as soon as rumours about his special demands for the new contract with Keystone reached other film companies. They tried to buy him by offering more than Keystone, but Charlie was determined about the amount he wanted as his salary.

At last, Essanay Studios came to him with a proposal which he could hardly refuse. It was more than he had asked for, and thus, as soon as he completed his last movie with Keystone, he joined Essanay at the end of 1914.

His Prehistoric Past, Charlie's final movie with Keystone, was released on December 7, 1914, and was set in the prehistoric times as the name suggests. In the movie, Charlie tried to kill the king of the tribe to take his place and his wife, which certainly was quite the opposite of what a character like the tramp would have normally done. So, much to the delight of the audience, in the end what happens is that Charlie wakes up in a park bench to realise that he was dreaming all along.

❑

Understanding the Tramp

Before Charlie became the tramp, he had been in theatre playing a variety of roles, having a very different costume. In *Making a Living*, which was his first movie, he wore a long droopy moustache, a top hat, and a frockcoat. He was a short man in reality, but in this particular guise, he looked rather tall, and it gave out a very different image of him; rich and overpowering, which the tramp was not.

Charlie's creation of the tramp was spontaneous as has already been established. He was still working on the character when he came out wearing the costume and showing it to Mr. Sennett. He wrote in his autobiography, "When I confronted Sennett, I assumed the character and strutted about, swinging my cane and parading before him... I began to explain the character: 'You know this fellow is many-sided, a tramp, a gentleman, a poet, a dreamer, a lonely fellow, always hopeful of romance and adventure. He would have you believe he is a scientist, a musician, a duke, a polo-player. However, he is not above picking up cigarette-butts or robbing a baby of its candy. And, of course, if the occasion warrants it, he will kick a lady in the rear – but only in extreme anger.'"[40]

Although Charlie made the tramp sound pitiable from the start, Sennett thought otherwise, "It was a long time before he abandoned cruelty, venality, treachery, larceny, and lechery as the main characteristics of the tramp. Chaplin shrank his tramp in gradually diminishing sizes and made him pathetic – and loveable."[41]

Charlie began working with Essanay from the beginning of 1915. They were set up in Niles and Chicago. Before moving to Niles, Charlie made one movie in Chicago, which was called *His New Job.*

Charlie brought with him to Essanay the character of the tramp, which was born on the sets of Keystone. It was his own creation and, hence, he was allowed to use it anywhere. He now played the tramp in almost every movie. He had chosen to play this character ever since the success of the first movie in which he had appeared as that. "As the clothes had imbued me with the character, I then and there decided I would keep to this costume, whatever happened."[42]

Mr. Anderson, the one with whom Charlie had all the talk, had promised him a huge salary owing to the success of the tramp's character. But when Charlie was making his first movie with Essanay, Mr. Spoor, the co-founder, was absent from the sets and two weeks had passed since and Charlie had not yet received his cheque. He got to know the reason behind this drama much later. Mr. Spoor did not trust Charlie's competence as he had never heard of him and was mad at Anderson for hiring him for an amount which they could not afford.

Apart from that, Charlie was also not happy with the work environment of Essanay. It was too uncreative and extremely formal, unlike the techniques of Keystone, where he had complete freedom to do whatever he wished.

When Spoor got to know about the popularity of Charlie Chaplin, he apologised to him and gave him the bonus and the cheques that Anderson had promised. The demand for Chaplin films had begun even before he made his first film with them, so Spoor was much amazed and realised that he had struck a goldmine.

From then on, Charlie got what he asked for. When he told Spoor that he wanted to shift to Niles, Spoor agreed.

Charlie met Edna Purviance while he was working in Niles. She was suggested to him by another actor who worked with Anderson. When he met her, she seemed very serious and aloof, yet Charlie hired her because he found her to be beautiful. "She would at least be decorative to my comedies."[43]

Edna proved to be more than just decorative for his movies. She, in fact, played the leading lady in many of Charlie's films and eventually became one of the most popular female actors in the film industry.

With Essanay, Charlie also made a movie called *The Tramp*. In this, Charlie played a kind of a hero who saves the lady, which is played by Edna, from a couple of crooks. She invites him to her farmland, where he is given a job by her father. "Here Charlie's lovelorenness is really just a way of ending the story and isn't brought to the forefront as it is to be later.... His switch of allegiance, decided by his colonization by the world of virtue (represented by Edna), is reminiscent of his similar conversion in *Police*, but in *The Tramp* it doesn't so pointedly emphasize as in the later film, his moral ambiguity, and so never starts to become a theme. Yet the excellent comedy that justifies one's thinking of *The Tramp* as, after all, a very fine film, is independent of these anticipations."[44]

As Sennett had pointed out, the tramp really did not have a full character until much later. Undoubtedly, he was full of ideas but in his previous movies, Charlie just used the tramp to do everything which normally could have been called as unacceptable by the society. He was playing a 'Fool', in the guise of a 'Hero'.

"Like the court jester or the Shakespearean fool, the tramp can point out society's idiosyncrasies without being persecuted. Not only is he not chastised for his critique on society, he is applauded with laughter."[45]

The tramp was a part of comedy movies and not dramatic ones even though he had all the qualities of making people cry. "I was playing in a picture called *The New Janitor*, in a scene in which the manager of the office fires me. In pleading with him to take pity on me and let me retain my job, I started to pantomime appealingly that I had a large family of little children. Although I was enacting mock sentiment, Dorothy Davenport, an old actress, was on the sidelines watching the scene, and during rehearsal, I looked up and to my surprise, found her in tears. 'I know it's supposed to be funny,' she said, 'but you just make me weep.' She confirmed something I already felt: I had the ability to evoke tears as well as laughter."[46]

Perhaps, this was the reason, why he happened to make full-length tragicomedies soon after he opened his own studio.

Currently, while Charlie was working with Essanay, he made only comedies where his tramp was mostly a shrewd opportunist or a lecherous being. But sometimes he was also a man with some morals. This happened when he started giving more thought to his plots. "The evolution of the Tramp was undoubtedly fuelled by Chaplin's efforts to seize greater creative control over his films. Unlike the Keystone comedies, which have simple plot and place a primacy on farce humor, Chaplin's Essanay comedies display more sophisticated plots and involve more textured characters. The maddening pace of producing nearly one new Keystone comedy each week was reflected in the rapid pace and formulaic story lines in the films. However, the pace at Essanay was somewhat slower, allowing Chaplin to take more time and care in creating his films, and more room to experiment. The tempered pace shows in the style of the films, which contain more subtle pantomime and character development. Although the first seven films Chaplin made for Essanay were released over three months, Chaplin slowed the pace of production to one two-reel film per month after that."[47]

After making a few movies in Niles, Charlie demanded that he needed better facilities. Anderson was reluctant as they did not have the means to build another studio. However, they managed to rent a small studio in Los Angeles, with which Charlie was much happy.

Charlie's movies were really doing well which cued Essanay to charge more money from the exhibitors, and, in the process, they profited much. Charlie got to know his true worth when suddenly one day he received a telegram from New York, which read as thus, "Will give Chaplin $25,000 for two weeks to appear fifteen minutes each evening at the New York Hippodrome. This will not interfere with his work."[48]

Anderson refused Charlie to go to New York for the two weeks and instead offered to give him that money, provided he made a two-reeler comedy soon. It was during this time that Charlie found out that products in his name are being merchandised all over the country and caricatures of his tramp are being sold in the form of little statues. Now, Charlie fully understood the market value that his name alone bore and, thus, started hatching better plans for his future.

In Los Angeles, Charlie was able to meet his brother more often, who had become quite successful by that time. Sydney now wanted to help Charlie, and had decided to join him as his unofficial manager, once his contract with Karno was over.

The moment Sydney began assisting his brother, the first thing he suggested Anderson was to change the distribution system and to make it more effective, so that they can earn maximum profit. This helped Essanay so much that Charlie began receiving a huge amount of bonus with every movie he made from then onwards.

When Charlie's contract was coming to an end, he tried negotiating with Spoor regarding increasing his salary by a huge percentage. But he did not entertain his argument and, thus, Charlie decided to leave Essanay at the end of the contract, without having any other job at hand.

What was going on in Charlie's mind at this point of time? "The future, the future – the wonderful future! Where was it leading? The prospects were dazzling. Like an avalanche, money and success came with increasing momentum; it was all bewildering, frightening – but wonderful."[49]

Then he met Nat Goodwin. He was a very popular American theatre actor and comedian. They became such good friends that whatever he told Charlie, the latter listened to them as good advice. "You've made a remarkable success, and there's a wonderful life ahead of you if you know how to handle yourself."[50] Nat was an aged man, married eight times and all his wives were very beautiful.

Charlie left for New York after his last movie with Essanay was completed. He was going to board a train which would take five days to reach the destination. He had informed Sydney all about how he was coming via a telegram post.

So, when his train stopped in Amarillo, Texas for some time, a crowd of people headed by the Mayor had gathered around, to welcome Charlie Chaplin to their town. How did they come to know about it? It seems that when Charlie had sent that telegram to Sydney, the telegraph operators read the message and decided to announce his travel plans to everybody. Thus, the same event took place in Kansas City and all the other towns where the train had to wait.

Charlie reached New York after what seemed a very long and tiresome journey, but when he met Sydney, all his other thoughts vanished after hearing the good news. He told Charlie that he had made a deal for him with the Mutual Film Corporation, which was ready to pay him an extremely high salary.

When all this was happening, Charlie did not seem to enjoy his fame. He was rather depressed, as he himself said, "It seemed that everyone knew me, but I knew no one; I became introspective, full of self-pity, and a spell of melancholy beset me."[51]

Working with Mutual

Charlie worked in Mutual for about two years during which time he made several movies on their set in Los Angeles. His tramp was now beginning to develop a character which had many sides to it. He was not just any 'Fool' now. He had progressed to become a 'Wise Fool'. He was the hero of his movies, but did not exactly have any heroic traits, except that he provided the audience with something which was lacking in Comedies before – a perspective.

"In his role as the vagabond, Chaplin represents an underdog that the audience can sympathize with.

As the underdog, he is overlooked by society. It is this status as outsider that is key to Chaplin's success at social commentary....

The character of the tramp continues to make people laugh. Chaplin's comedies combine serious social issues with humorous situations creating a plethora of avenues for the tramp to do what he does best. The tramp is naively ingenious in his ability to ascertain society's loopholes, physically adept at escaping society's traps, and above all else, the tramp is a hero to society's outcasts."[52]

Why was the tramp always posing as the outcast? Probably, this question could be answered by the fact that Charlie was always attracted towards the real heroes of theatre, the ones which never featured as the hero on stage. "Of the many artists I saw as a child, those who impressed me the most were not always the successful ones but those with unique personalities off stage."[53]

While the characterisations of the movies were becoming complicated, the time that each movie took to be made also increased. Most of the time, Charlie used to be stuck with the plot, not knowing what to do next. At such times, he just wandered about on the film set doing nothing, but internally, he was trying to find his answers. To an onlooker, it looked as if he was whiling away his time, but only Charlie knew the torment that he was going through in his mind.

The Vagabond which was released on July 10, 1916, was one of Charlie's most famous movies produced by Mutual. It had Charlie as a violist and Edna as the lost child of a rich family, who was brought up by gypsies. Charlie rescues Edna from those people and brings her to a safer place. One day, when an artist, taken in by her beauty, draws a portrait of hers, she is soon found by her mother, who comes and takes her home.

"This is Charlie's version of pastoral. Everybody who has written or thought about the film recognizes that it has a special atmosphere that sets it apart from the other films of the period, and that this distinction has to do both with its unusual rural setting and with the feelings of love and the loss of love with which the action deals. It is Chaplin's first thoroughgoing essay in the comedy of feeling, in which the feelings in question predominate and ask to be taken seriously.... It seems to me to be the first of the three unquestionable masterpieces of Chaplin's Mutual period.... What can easily be missed, and has not so far as I know been remarked on, is that in addition to the pastoral theme and the love theme, the film has an art theme. It dramatizes two conflicting conceptions of art in a way that relates it to *The Circus* quite as strongly as the Charlie-Edna-Artist triangle.... Charlie's practice of art as a function continuous with life is beautifully expressed in the scene of his serenading of Edna."[54]

Some of the other popular movies of Charlie with Mutual were *The Champion*, *The Fireman*, *The Pawnshop*, *The Immigrant* and *The Rink*.

Charlie was gradually becoming involved with issue-based movies. His *The Immigrant*, released on June 17, 1917, was quite a film having this aspect. John Kimber, in his book, gives his opinion on this movie, "It appears to offer itself as a realistic rendering of the experience of the impoverished European immigrant to the United States at the time of the greatest influx. It has relevance, even authority, as a social document, and may well have been based upon Charlie's personal observation. But its realistic status is qualified in a variety of ways; and its centre of interest, as often with Chaplin, is quite as much a generalised human predicament, which it does not take special knowledge to sympathise with." Then he goes on to talk about the movie's plot and the love story between Charlie and Edna which ends happily, except for the last shot where, "the bureau official's face, impenetrably severe and bald, hints at the hardships the immigrants have still to meet."[55]

On Charlie's sets, no one ever got hurt, and he made sure of that. Whatever fight scenes were there in his movies, they were choreographed and, hence, actors did not actually have to hit or slap each other. "We had only one accident in the whole series. It happened in *Easy Street.* While I was pulling a street-lamp over the big bully to gas him, the head of the lamp collapsed and its sharp metal edge fell across the bridge of my nose, necessitating to surgical stitches."[56]

When Charlie's contract with Mutual was coming to an end, he was twenty-seven and single and on the verge of becoming a millionaire. He was one of the most eligible bachelors in the country at that time, and yet he felt quite lonely sometimes. Maybe it was time for him to have a companion in his life.

Much has been spoken about Charlie's friendship with Douglas Fairbanks and many say that they first met in front of a movie poster of Fairbanks, which Charlie happened to see at the same time when Fairbanks was there, and that without recognising, both were talking ill of each other, not knowing who the other actually was.

But Charlie claims otherwise. He wrote in his autobiography that one night Fairbanks was hosting a party at his house and Charlie was forced by one of his friends to go to it. When he reached, Fairbanks himself tried to hide by going into another room.

Charlie said that was the night when they became friends for life.

Both Charlie and Fairbanks had achieved great heights in their career and their friendship was blooming. Charlie did not feel lonely anymore as most of his time, he spent staying with his new friend at his bungalow in Beverly Hills. Fairbanks was soon married to Mary Pickford, who was quite a famous movie actor and had a huge fan following of her own. Their marriage lasted for about fifteen years and ended finally in 1936.

Working with First National

Now was the time when Charlie was moving on to a whole new level. As someone rightly said, "When Charlie joined the Keystone Company in December 1913, he was a novice in the art of making comic films. When he left the Mutual Company in July 1917, he was a veteran whose finest work was still to come. In between he made some 61 films, excluding a number of unauthorised compilations."[57]

The news of Charlie's contract with the First National has a funny incident behind it. One day, while he was in his room, Sydney busted in and told him about an over-million-dollar contract, which the First National wanted him to sign. As he was delivering this piece of news, he noticed that Charlie was wearing only a towel and holding a violin, playing *The Tales of Hoffmann*. The situation seemed so funny that Sydney instantly decided to put this image in his memoirs.

Charlie worked with First National for a period of four years, starting 1918. During this time, Charlie decided to squander some of his money as he had not realised until then what good money felt like; so he went to a showroom one day and bought a car. He even kept a secretary after realising that he was not able to handle all his affairs by himself anymore. Not knowing what to do with the rest of the money, he asked Sydney to help him to invest them. Sydney was only too happy to help his brother.

Charlie had to begin from scratch at First National, as they did not even have a studio. He helped them to build one and while it was being made, he took a short vacation with Edna Purviance. Yes, she was romantically involved with him to an extent that Charlie once even thought of marrying her. But he soon put that thought aside as he could not think of one reason why he should take her as his wife. They eventually became 'good friends' and she found someone else for herself.

The first film that Charlie made with First National was *A Dog's Life.* Here the tramp had a real character. The name itself suggests the pathetic nature of the situation. "As a tale of mean streets and mean lives, *A Dog's Life* is a natural development from the great Mutual shorts. Its opening image of Charlie huddled miserably in the corner of a vacant lot is familiar and central. But although Charlie is shown as unjustly oppressed by our world in its harshest form, his relation to this world is not a simple one. For one thing, he is not just paraded for our pity.... Charlie's relation to our world is most precisely defined in the figure of Scraps. Scraps is the film's central image, and its most important addition to the typical situation.... For Charlie, Scraps is not a pet but a pal... As much as a fable of social deprivation, *A Dog's Life* is a film about balance and mastery – about Charlie's precarious possession of our world, and his efforts to maintain it."[58]

Then Charlie made *Shoulder Arms* (October 1918). War had taken a toll on everyone, and it was four years since its commencement; America was beginning to get affected by it. So Charlie thought, "Why not a comedy about the war?"[59] The central theme behind *Shoulder Arms* was war. Here, Charlie's character of the tramp is seen as the hero who helps the 'good' side to win the war by capturing Kaiser.

"The tree impersonation sequence is one of the film's boldest strokes. It has a multiple function. It's obvious, if ludicrous purpose is to provide Charlie the infiltrator with adequate camouflage. But its very absurdity also, in the way I've suggested, provides Charlie the character with protection against too serious an involvement with the realities of war. It establishes the fantastic nature of the involvement we are to expect, and serves as a suitable prologue to the even more fantastic events that follow."[60]

After the film was completed, Charlie was not much satisfied, as he had intended to make a longer film, but ended up cutting some parts from the script, because of the problems of production cost and other such things.

Shoulder Arms turned out to be a great success and had become quite popular among the soldiers. Fairbanks came out with tears down his cheeks from its screening, and those tears were but of laughter.

And then the war ended in November 1918 to everyone's relief, and as Charlie expressed in his autobiography, "Living without war was like being suddenly released from prison."[61]

Charlie's one of the most celebrated movies was made with First National. *The Kid* was as commercially appealing as it could get. "*The Kid* consists of a comic drama of Charlie's relation with Jackie set within a sentimental one of Edna's loss and recovery of her son.... It shares with the Charlie-Jackie story a situation that demonstrates the vulnerability of affectionate relationships."[62]

The Kid (February 1921) was one of the very few movies which did not have Charlie, the tramp, romancing any lady. Although in the end he does enter Edna's house, yet it was only the child that Charlie desired to be with.

It is an interesting story about how Charlie ended up making this movie. He was anxious to find a good story and was exhausted with his personal life. He had just completed *Sunnyside* (June 1919) and was not happy with it. He wanted to do something bigger than he had ever done, but there was no inspiration. Then one day, he saw a child dancing in a theatre along with his father. He had never seen a child so small and yet so confident. His name was Jackie Coogan.

The idea for this film did not immediately strike him. It was not until a couple of weeks later when he heard that Coogan was hired by some company, that he desired to have the child in his movie. Ideas started crawling in to his mind but there was no way that he could do anything about it now. Then someone on the set came up to Charlie, announcing that it was Coogan Sr., who had been hired by the other company. A new wave of excitement flowed through the set. Charlie at once called the father and asked to meet him.

Coogan was too excited and gave his permission to hire his son for any number of movies that he wanted; and after his own contract was over, he came up to Charlie's set and helped out with the management of his son.

Charlie was too happy with Jackie's performance and praises him in the autobiography. "There is a scene in *The Kid* where the boy is about to throw a stone at a window. A policeman steals up behind him, and, as he brings his hand back to throw, it touches the policeman's coat. He looks up at the policeman, then playfully tosses the stone up and catches it, then innocently throws it away and ambles off, suddenly busting into a sprint.... The scene was one of Jackie's best, and was one of the high spots in the picture."[63]

The Kid also got its share of criticism. For instance, J.M. Barrie once asked Charlie:

"'Why did you interpose a dream sequence in *The Kid*? It interrupted the flow of the story.' 'Because I was influenced by *A Kiss for Cinderella*', I answered frankly."[64]

Some of the other movies which he made with First National are *The Idle Class*, *The Pilgrim*, *A Day's Pleasure*, *Pay Day* and a few more.

Humour in the Absurd

"There was pathos to the Little Tramp, yet he really did not want to be pitied."[65]

The tramp was many things, but he did not require anyone's sympathy. This Charlie had clearly established since his first appearance in that role. At first, he freely kicked anyone in their arse and did not even have to apologise. A friend of Charlie Judge Henshaw had once commented, "What I like about your comedy is your knowledge of fundamentals – you know that the most undignified part of a man's anatomy is his arse, and your comedies prove it."[66]

Gradually, the tramp became modest, less lecherous and more lovable. Since he belonged to the lower strata of the society, he started looking miserable as soon as he started having feelings.

"In the Keystone days the tramp had been freer and less confined to plot. His brain was seldom active then – only his instincts, which were concerned with the basic essentials: food, warmth and shelter. But with each succeeding comedy, the tramp was growing more complex. Sentiment was beginning to percolate through the character."[67]

Charlie admits that the complexity of the tramp made his movies more difficult to be made. It took more time, now that he needed all his shots to complement each other. He had grown a lot in the movie business and was now making feature length movies, having better plots and stories.

In *The Kid*, when the child is taken away from Charlie, a lump forms in the throats of the viewers, because they feel more involved. Then Charlie's chasing of the van in order to unite with the child, whom he had taken care of since the day he picked him up from road, is the most moving. The audience wants him to save the child and doesn't want him to be with his mother. They forget the mother's love and do not sympathise with her, simply because they have decided that Charlie deserves him more.

Whatever the tramp wanted, he always got, and hence, no matter however pathetic he looked, he never felt any shame in it.

When Charlie was little, he had come across an incident, which happened to inspire many of his comedies. "At the end of our street was a slaughter-house, and sheep would pass our house on their way to be butchered. I remember one escaped and ran down the street to the amusement of onlookers. Some tried to grab it and others tripped over themselves. I had giggled with delight at its lambent capering and panic, it seemed so comic. But when it was caught and carried back into the slaughter-house, the reality of the tragedy came over me and I ran indoors, screaming and weeping to Mother: 'They're going to kill it! They're going to kill it!' That stark, spring afternoon and that comedy chase stayed with me for days; and I wonder if that episode did not establish the premise of my future films – the combination of the tragic and the comic."[68]

This is why Charlie's humour was very different from most of the comedies of that time. He sent out a message in every tragicomedy that he made. He believed that through humour in serious situations, he could make anyone go beyond their own thought process.

"For instance, at a funeral where friends and relatives are gathered in hushed reverence around the bier of the departed, a late arrival enters just as the service is about to begin and hurriedly tiptoes to his sear, where one mourner has left his top hat. In his hurry, the late arrival accidentally sits on it, then with a solemn look of mute apology, he hands it crushed to its owner, who takes it with mute annoyance and continues listening to the service. And solemnity of the moment becomes ridiculous."[69]

This little story does not just make a person laugh, but also makes them ponder at the uselessness of the societal norms. Society demands a certain standard from people in their behaviour, and Charlie ridicules it through his movies. The Wise Fool speaks silently and mocks the society for its absurdity. And that is the reason, why the tramp doesn't need any pity.

❑

Chaplin's Techniques

Saying that Charlie had a unique technique by which he made films, would be going a little overboard. He used the same camera, same kind of sets, same musical instruments and same actors. Yet, what was so different about his films which the audience loved?

It's not that the other filmmakers were not good. There was a huge fan following and a very large audience for actors such as Douglas Fairbanks, Buster Keaton, John Barrymore, Gary Cooper, Greta Garbo, Mary Pickford, and the movies made by D.W. Griffith, Sergei Eisenstein[70] and others.

Charlie used something else which was only unique to him: his passion. It was a little after he became popular that he developed an obsession to keep up to his standards. His movies became lengthier, more character specific, having better stories and the time taken to complete each movie also augmented. It was this passion that helped him achieve that legendary height, where he is now.

After a few movies, people started calling his camera techniques as old fashioned. In reply to this, he had written, "My technique is the outcome of thinking for myself, of my own logic and approach; it is not borrowed from what others are doing."[71]

He also had a very distinctive way of handling his crew members. Whenever someone new joined in, he tried to make him feel as involved as possible by asking him to give his opinion about a particular shot or something. This helped the newcomer to drop their guard and, in this way, a special bond was created.

Charlie was an idealist and believed that only a free mind is able to create a beautiful piece of art. "To an artist complete freedom to do the unorthodox is usually most exciting, and this is why many a director's first picture has freshness and originality."[72]

Perhaps, it was also the character of the 'Tramp' that helped Charlie, along with his passion. The tramp is the most important part of his movies. It features in almost every movie that he has ever made, and the reason has already been established.

There was not much technique involved with the tramp. The audience loved him, probably because his image reflected their own. One must not forget the time in which Charlie made movies. It was the time of the Great Depression, and the two World Wars; when the entire world was in turmoil – socially, politically and economically. Whether the tramp was its deliberate reproduction or an innocent development, one cannot tell; because no one can really decipher the ways in which a mind works.

The Importance of Music in His Movies

"There is nothing so warm and moving as the sight of a symphony orchestra. The romantic lights of their music stands, the tuning up and the sudden silence as the conductor makes his entrance, affirms the social, cooperative feeling."[73]

Music in any movie is important to set one's mood. Especially, in silent movies, it also plays the role of expressing oneself. Almost every movie of Charlie is incomplete without such soulful music. "An old song called *Mrs. Grundy* created the mood for *The Immigrant*. The tune had a wistful tenderness that suggested two lonely derelicts getting married on a doleful, rainy day."[74]

Charlie had learnt how to play violin and cello when he came to America with Karno's Company. He used to ask the musician to give him lessons in between his shows. It helped Charlie to develop an ear for tunes, and later, to even compose some of his own music for the movies.

Charlie was first acquainted with the magic of music when he was living with his father for some time. "It came from the vestibule of the White Hart corner pub, and resounded brilliantly in the empty square. The tune was *The Honeysuckle and the Bee*, played with radiant virtuosity on a harmonium and clarinet. I had never been conscious of melody before, but this one was beautiful and lyrical, so blithe and gay, so warm and reassuring."[75]

Probably, that melody attracted his state of mind at that time, or maybe it was just too melodic for him to ignore. Nonetheless, the point is, that day, Charlie understood what music really meant; it had appealed to his soul. He later realised that it was not just the melodic tunes, but its combination with the sound effects which created more magic.

How He Got His Ideas for the Plot

Charlie was often asked how he got ideas for his movies. "By sheer perseverance to the point of madness"[76] was his answer.

He had admitted in his autobiography that he usually started with just one idea and extended it to create the story. "I would say, pick a subject that will stimulate you, elaborate it and involve it, then, if you can't develop it further, discard it and pick another. Elimination from accumulation is the process of finding what you want."[77]

But in his later movies, when he was making feature length movies, all his shots needed to be balanced with each other and for that, one thought wouldn't have worked. Hence, that was when more planning and more resources were needed and Charlie's one-man show came to an end.

How He Got the Girls to Like the Tramp

Tramp was a pathetic character in the later movies. He was sad, poor and had a little self-esteem. He stopped looking at women lecherously, and yet, in the end, he still got the heroine. How was it possible? "Logically it was difficult to get a beautiful girl interested in a tramp. This has always been a problem in my films. In *The Gold Rush* the girl's interest in the tramp started by her playing a joke on him, which later moves her to pity, which he mistakes for love. The girl in *City Lights* is blind. In this relationship, he was romantic and wonderful to her until her sight is restored."[78]

His Art Form

Charlie's art portrayed individualism; his ideas were so self-contained that if one tried to confine him into a small box, he would still find something to do in it. As John Kimber, in his book, explained, "His clowning is spontaneous, self-sufficient and intimate.... While other clown's gags, however brilliant, bear a stamp of lengthy calculation, Charlie's simply happen, presenting themselves to us with all the immediacy of life.... When you look at it, the self-sufficiency of Charlie's comedy derives partly from the fact that so much of it involves only the use of his own person, or of articles of his costume. His face is obviously one of his most valuable instruments."[79]

Charlie's works were a reproduction of his own convictions. He made what he liked and trusted the audience to understand him.

He had faith in the art of pantomime and believed that there was no need to say things when actions could speak better. Hence, when sound was introduced, he did everything he could to keep his art form alive. In all the hype around the talkies, Charlie made some of the best silent movies ever. Although when he eventually did make talkies, they too were phenomenal.

Charlie did not get much pleasure in watching Shakespearean plays. "I cannot pretend to enjoy Shakespeare in the theatre.... I feel I am listening to a scholarship oration."[80]

He was anyway not a fan of dialogues, but the language in Shakespeare's plays was so difficult, that Charlie concluded that it was not for the general audience. He also did not like themes that he chose to write on. "In my pursuit of bread and cheese, honour was seldom trafficked in. I cannot identify myself with a prince's problems."[81]

What he overlooked here was the fact that in Shakespeare's time, that dialect was the normal way of speaking among the people; and to write about Royal families was how the writers survived. Sure, Shakespeare today cannot be understood outside a classroom, but that doesn't mean they are not for everyone. His art form was different from Shakespeare's, and there is no doubt about it, but one cannot be compared to the other.

Charlie, throughout his profession, learnt two most important things about acting. He first realised that the key to great acting was having a relaxed mind. He wrote this in his autobiography, in the section where he tries to tell his readers about the techniques required in making movies. "How does one relax? That is difficult. My own method is rather personal: before going on the stage, I am always extremely nervous and excited, and in this state, I get so exhausted that by the time I make my entrance, I am relaxed."[82]

The second most important thing which he discovered was that acting could not be taught, and that it was crucial that one had emotions. "All intellect and no feeling can be characteristic of the arch-criminal, and all feeling and no intellect exemplify the harmless idiot. But when intellect and feeling are perfectly balanced, then we get the superlative actor."[83]

Charlie's methods only he knew best. But one thing is for certain; he was indeed very special. To be a great actor is in itself a challenge; to direct good movies is another. But to create a character, which stays in the hearts of everyone forever, is something beyond extraordinary.

❑

Visiting Europe

"For seven years, I have been basking in California's perpetual sunlight, a sunlight artificially enhanced by the studio Cooper-Hewitts. For seven years I have been working and thinking along in a single channel and I wanted to get away. Away from Hollywood, the cinema colony, away from scenarios, away from the celluloid smell of the studios, away from contracts, press notices, cutting rooms, crowds, bathing beauties, custard pies, big shoes, and little moustaches. I was in the atmosphere of achievement, but an achievement which, to me, was rapidly verging on stagnation. I wanted an emotional holiday."[84]

It was in the year 1921 that Charlie revisited his past. To him it was a wistful experience because it was after seven long years that he was coming back to England. Although he did not wish to stay there, he still had some wonderful memories, which he intended to recollect by walking down the streets of London.

He had decided to remain in America for the rest of his life. He wasn't an American citizen, at least not officially, but he always felt that he belonged there.

So, when he returned to London, it was only a short visit. He wished to meet some of his friends, including Hetty Kelly, and take a small vacation around Europe, relax for a while, and then go back and complete his contact with the First National. Before leaving America, he heard that Hetty Kelly had died, which depressed him a little.

"On the train journey to London, he found everything different and irresistibly beautiful, the girls, the countryside – despite the parched grass and the new buildings – the crowds that waited at every station to see his train go by.... The scenes that awaited him in London were astonishing. His homecoming was a triumph hardly paralleled in the twentieth century apart from a few great royal or national events. From Waterloo to the Ritz, the streets were thronged with people all waiting for a glimpse of their idol and a chance to cheer."[85]

When Charlie arrived in London, he was a little upset because of the crowd. He had wanted some peace and quiet, but all he got were people surrounding him, asking him to say a few words to the public, journalists requiring interviews and friends wanting to spend some time with him. When he reached his hotel, he made an excuse about desiring to take a nap, so that his friends leave him alone.

What he did after that resonates a beautiful image of an afternoon's adventure of a child. "As soon as they had gone, I hurriedly changed my clothes, took the freight elevator and left unnoticed by the back entrance. Immediately I made my way down Jermyn Street, hired a taxi and was off, down the Haymarket, through Trafalgar Square, down Parliament Street and over Westminster Bridge. The taxi turned a corner, and, at last, Kennington Road!"[86]

Charlie wanted to visit all the places in Kennington Road, which he was acquainted with. He saw the window of his old room in Pownall Terrace, and the house where he lived with his father, and also visited the bank where he had first opened his account when he had started working. "That visit to Kennington, 3 Pownall Terrace, had completed something within me."[87]

While in America, when Charlie had finished making *The Idle Class* and was exhausted, he had received a letter from the famous science-fiction writer, H.G. Wells, who had expressed his desire to meet him. It was then that Charlie decided to take a trip to Europe thinking that it would be a good break. This tour was one beautiful memory for Charlie, as he got to visit not only his past, but also meet many legendary personalities.

Among them was Sir James Matthew Barrie, the author of *Peter Pan*. Charlie was attending a party, where he met Sir Barrie and was obliged when the latter invited him to his house for a meeting.

"Barrie's apartment was like an atelier, a large room with a beautiful view of the river Thames. In the centre of the room was a round stove with a chimney-pipe ascending to the ceiling. He took us to a window that looked out on a narrow side-street with a window directly opposite. 'That's Shaw's[88] bedroom,' he said mischievously with his Scotch accent. 'When I see a light on, I flip cherry-stones or plum-stones at the window. If he wants to chat, he opens it and we do a little back-yard gossiping, and, if he doesn't, then he pays no attention or turns out the light. Usually, I flip out three times, then give up.'"[89]

Then Charlie met with H.G. Wells. They had a rather serious talk about Russia and the issuing of manifestoes. "Organization is needed, he says, and is just as important as disarmament. Education is the only salvation, not only of Russia, but of the rest of the world. Socialism of the right sort will come through proper education."[90] Charlie told him that his knowledge on Socialism was limited and that he "saw little virtue in a system in which man must work to live."[91]

Many people have accused Charlie of being a Communist. But with that comment about Socialism and that thought on the system of 'work to live' could hardly have made Charlie a Communist.

Charlie also had a deep desire to meet Thomas Burke, the author of *Limehouse Nights*. He felt that they both were similar in many ways.

"London and its experiences are telling on me and I am nervous and unstrung. I must see Burke and go with him alone. He is the one man who sees London through the same kind of glasses as myself. I am told that Burke will be disappointing because he is so silent, but I do not believe that I will be disappointed in him."[92]

Charlie describes his meeting with Thomas Burke in his book *My Trip Abroad*.

"As Burke and I ramble along towards no place in particular, I talk about his book. I have read 'Limehouse Nights' as he wrote it. There is nothing I could see half so effective. We discuss the fact that realities such as he has kept alive seldom happen in a stroll, but I am satisfied. I don't want to see. It could not be more beautiful than the book. There is no reaction to my flattery. I must watch good taste. Passing up my obvious back-patting, I feel that he is very intelligent, and I am silent for quite a while as we stroll along towards Stepney. There is a greenish mist hanging about everything and we seem to be in a labyrinth of narrow alleyways, now turning into streets and then merging into squares. He is silent and we merely walk.

And then I awaken. I see his purpose. I can do my own story, he is merely lending me the tools. And what tools they are! I feel that I have served an ample apprenticeship in their use, through merely reading his stories. I am fortified. It is so easy now. He has given me the stories before.

Now he is telling them over in pictures. The very shadows take on life and romance. The skulking, strutting, mincing, hurrying forms that pass us and fade out into the night are now becoming characters. The curtain has risen on 'Limehouse Nights', dramatized with the original cast."[93]

Charlie's next stop was Paris. He had wished to see the beauty that surrounded the romantic city. But as soon as he reached, there was a huge crowd and he had no free time left for himself. "It has started to rain as we arrive in Paris, which adds to my state of excitement, and a reportorial avalanche falls upon me. I am about to overcome. How did reporters know I was coming? The crowd outside the station is almost as large as the one in London."[94]

Next day, Charlie had lunch with Waldo Frank and Dudley Field Malone. Later, he walked on the streets of Paris with Waldo, which he described as thus:

"Waldo Frank and I sit on a bench in the Champs Elysees and watch the wagons going to market in the early morning. Paris seems most beautiful to me just at this time. What a city! What is the force that has made it what it is? Could anyone conceive such a creation, such a land of continuous gayety? It is a masterpiece among cities, the last word in pleasure. Yet I feel that something has happened to it, something that they are trying to cover by heightened plunges into song and laughter. We stroll along the boulevard and it is growing light. I am recognized and we are being followed. We are passing a church. There is an old woman asleep on the steps, but she does not seem worn and haggard. There is almost a smile on her face as she sleeps. She typifies Paris to me. Hides her poverty behind a smile."[95]

In France, Charlie also met with some eminent personalities like Sir Philip Sassoon, Lloyd George, Lord and Lady Rock-Savage and Lady Diana Manners.

Then Charlie went to Germany. It surprised him when he reached the city that almost no one recognised him. He was told that nobody in Germany had seen his films, which explained a lot.

In Berlin, Charlie met Pola Negri, who was a Polish actress. It was only after she recognised him, that Charlie got some attention in the country. "Pola Negri is really beautiful.... Beautiful jet-black hair, white, even teeth and wonderful coloring. I think it such a pity that such coloring does not register on the screen. She is the center of attraction here. I am introduced. What a voice she has! Her mouth speaks so prettily the German language. Her voice has a soft, mellow quality, with charming inflections. Offered a drink, she clinks my glass and offers her only English words, 'Jazz boy Charlie.'"[96]

Charlie really loved the country at his first glance. The fact that they were their enemy did not much bother him. He, in fact, overlooked that part and grasped its true beauty. He wrote the following about it in his book, "Germany is beautiful. Germany belies the war. There are people crowding the fields, tilling the soil, working feverishly all the time as our train rushes through men, women and children are all at work. They are facing their problem and rebuilding.... The different style of architecture here is interesting. Factories are being built everywhere. Surely this isn't a conquered territory. I do not see much livestock in the fields."[97]

It was time for him to leave now. He came back to London and stayed there for a few days before moving on to America. When he looked back, he realised that he had made some really good friends.

Upon coming back from Germany, he had stayed with H.G. Wells, in his house and got acquainted with his whole family. Wells ended up becoming a lifelong friend to Charlie. "As I speed into town, I am wondering if Wells wants to know me or whether he wants me to know him. I am certain that now I have met Wells, really met him, more than I've met anyone in Europe. It's so worthwhile."[98]

He came back to America, eager to finish his contract with the First National. He had to make two more movies with them. Out of the two, *The Pilgrim* turned out to be a huge success as it had a deeper message than it really showed. "*The Pilgrim*, its serious preoccupations notwithstanding, is rooted in a very real world. We can't fail to notice that its metaphysical drama is acted out in terms of Charlie's worldliest concerns: money, food and women. And the actuality of its images is one of its most striking features. There is a fine appropriateness in faces, figures, dress, buildings and furnishings that gives substance to the film's definition of its themes.... The social context of the drama is rendered with a realism unusual for Chaplin (and, in the case of Edna's household, with real affection). Its blend of ironic comedy, moral complexity and visual reality makes *The Pilgrim* not only perhaps Chaplin's finest First National but one of the finest of all his films."[99]

In the end of the film, the Tramp is shown as running towards the horizon, having each foot at either side of the border. The significance of this scene can be read as that the tramp never really had any place which he could call as his home; but the fact he belonged to the whole world says a lot about his films cutting across all the borders of humanity.

❑

United Artists

Around the end of the second decade of the twentieth century, there was a conspiracy going on against the actors in the movie business. Charlie's success had led him to ask for a raise from the producers of First National, but when they hushed him up, he began suspecting that something was wrong. Similar incidents were being heard of from other actors. Fairbanks too confirmed with Charlie that his company was up to something.

Consequently, Charlie and the others hired a detective to go around with the producers and observe what was happening. The detective came back bearing a piece of news which worried them. She told them that the producers were planning to form a merger and tie up all the exhibitors of United States with a five-year contract. This, they deduced, would end the actor's rule in the industry.

Then Sydney came up with a plan. He suggested that if a few top grossing actors and directors announce their intention to stay separate from the producers and decide to sell their productions in the open market, they could defeat the producers' merger.

"It was not our intention to go through with this project, however. Our objective was only to stop exhibitors from signing a five-year contract with this proposed merger, for without the stars it would be worthless. We decided that the night before their convention we would appear together in the main dining-room of the Alexandria Hotel for dinner, and then make an announcement to the Press.

On that night Mary Pickford, D.W. Griffith, W.S. Hart, Douglas Fairbanks and myself sat on a table in the main dining-room. The effect was electric.... Very soon half a dozen members of the Press were sitting at our table taking notes as we issued our statement that we were forming a company of United Artists to protect our independence and to combat the forthcoming big merger. The story received front-page coverage."[100]

What happened after that is history. Producers from everywhere came up to them suggesting that they wanted to join them. They were even ready to settle for a small salary. "After such a reaction, we decided to go through with our project."[101]

Thus, the United Artists was established in this way by early 1919, although Charlie could not join them before the end of his contract with First National. He was to make six more movies with them before he could leave them for good.

When he finally completed those movies, it was already 1923.

The first movie that Charlie made with United Artists was *A Woman of Paris*, starring Edna Purviance. Previously, Charlie had intended to make his own version of *The Trojan Women*, but it wasn't working out. Then he wondered for some time about a story involving Josephine and Napoleon. He really wanted to make a film for Edna. But the more he thought about Napoleon, he strayed from his original plan of making a movie about Josephine. He ultimately had to put that project aside.

Meanwhile, Peggy Hopkins Joyce had come to Hollywood. She was a French woman with an astounding beauty but she was notorious for marrying five wealthy men for their money. Charlie had an affair with her but it did not last long. "During our bizarre, though brief, relationship Peggy told me several anecdotes about her association with a well-known French publisher. These inspired me to write the story *A Woman of Paris* for Edna Purviance to star in. I had no intention of appearing in the film but I directed it."[102]

Charlie had a tough time making this movie. He wanted to make something really different this time, something that no one had ever attempted before. "Some of the well-known effects of *A Woman of Paris* are now largely of historical interest: the rendering of the departing train solely in terms of shadow and light passing across Marie's face is in all the textbooks, but it takes an effort of imagination now to see it as a bold innovation, so thoroughly has it passed into the 'language'."[103]

Charlie also wanted to illustrate psychology on the big screen, and that too, without saying a single word. "Some critics declared that psychology could not be expressed on the silent screen, that obvious action, such as heroes bending ladies over tree-trunks and breathing fervently down into their tonsils, or chair-swinging, knock-out rough stuff, was its only means of expression."[104]

The film turned out to be a great success but only for a selective audience. Nonetheless, it started a rage and other directors soon decided to make movies of such character; and then suddenly, Hollywood had an outpour of films having psychology as its basic theme.

Charlie remained a member of the United Artists for the rest of his life and made some of his best movies while there.

Hannah's Last Years

After the completion of *The Kid*, and the end of the war, Charlie was able to bring his mother from England. "I had not seen her since I was last in England, a period of ten years, so I was somewhat shocked when a little old lady stepped off the train at Pasadena. She recognised Sydney and me at once and was quite normal."[105]

While she was healthy now, her mind never fully recovered. Charlie and Sydney had arranged for their mother to live in a house with a married couple who took care of her. They often came to visit her, and sometimes, even she came to Charlie's studio, where he would run some of his comedies for her.

This went on for quite a number of years, until she became physically ill, and when Charlie was filming *The Circus*, he received an urgent message regarding her second gall-bladder attack. "She had suffered a previous gall-bladder attack and had recovered. This time the doctors warned me that her relapse was serious. She had been taken to Glendale Hospital, but the doctors thought it advisable not to operate because of the weak condition of her heart."[106]

When Charlie went to meet her, she was only half conscious of what was happening in her surroundings. Nevertheless, he tried talking to her and she responded weakly. The next day, while Charlie was working, he got the news of her death. He was prepared for it, as the doctors had already told him about her condition.

"I stopped work, took off my make-up, and with Harry Crocker, my assistant director, went to the hospital.... Even in death, her expression looked troubled, as though anticipating further woes to come. How strange that her life should end here, in the environs of Hollywood, with all its absurd values – seven thousand miles from Lambeth, the soil of her heart-break. Then a flood of memories surged in upon me of her lifelong struggle, her suffering, her courage and her tragic, wasted life...and I wept."[107]

Charlie's last thought of her mother was a beautiful one. He did not want to remember her mother as someone who suffered, but as someone who made her children's lives worth living. "And in spite of the squalor in which we were forced to live, she had kept Sydney and me off the streets and made us feel we were not the ordinary product of poverty, but unique and distinguished."[108]

❑

The First Two Wives

Charlie had hired a new secretary, Tom Harrington. Within a few weeks, he realised that Tom was the best secretary he ever had. "He would call in the morning at the Athletic Club[109] with my mail and the newspapers and order my breakfast. Occasionally without comment he would leave books by my bedside.... He never spoke unless spoken to and had the gift of effacing himself while I had breakfast."[110]

It was in 1917, during the time when Charlie was working for Mutual, that he met Mildred Harris. Their first meeting did not leave any impression of Charlie, but when she kept calling him, and displayed her desire to spend time with him, that he suddenly became fond of her.

Tom Harrington played a distinct role in this affair. He tried to keep Charlie away from all media and when Mildred claimed that she was pregnant, that piece of news too did not affect Charlie's career. Charlie intended to marry her and they did. But it happened so fast and so mysteriously, that not many people came to know about it, until they were already married.

"On that day, I worked late at the studio. At seven-thirty, Tom came quietly on the set and whispered, 'Don't forget you have an appointment at eight.'... Then, he explained that I was to meet Miss Harris at the house of Mr. Sparks, the local registrar. When we arrived there, Mildred was seated in the hall.... Harrington quickly fumbled a ring into my hand as a tall, lean man appeared, warm and congenial, and ushered us into another room. It was Mr. Sparks. 'Well, Charlie,' he said, 'you certainly have a remarkable secretary. I didn't know it was to be you until half an hour ago.'"[111]

It is said that Charlie married Mildred after she claimed that she was pregnant with his child, although later he found out that it was a false alarm.

Their marriage lasted for two long and dreadful years. In the first year, Mildred gave birth to Charlie's first child, but it died after three days. This was the last strand in their knot, after which nothing helped them.

Charlie had never loved her. She was young and beautiful, but there was no match. The break-up with Edna had been recent when Charlie married Mildred. Some say that she was a rebound, but nothing could have been said for sure about why he actually married her. Thus, it was inevitable that they break up.

But this split came at a time when Charlie was working on *The Kid*. He had not yet finished cutting the film. Now, why did this divorce become a problem for Charlie?

"We separated in a friendly way, agreeing that she was to get the divorce on the grounds of mental cruelty, and that we would say nothing about it to the Press.... But she came out with a blast on the front page, saying that I had deserted her and that she was seeking a divorce on the grounds of mental cruelty."[112]

As a result of this, Charlie's completion of *The Kid* also became a big question mark. He had made a seven-reel feature film but First National wanted to release it as three two-reel comedies. Charlie definitely did not agree with them, also because in this way, he would have gotten lesser money for the whole film. "Legally they had little chance and they knew it. Therefore, they decided to operate through Mildred and try to attach *The Kid*."[113]

This was the cue for Charlie to pack his five hundred film-rolls of *The Kid* and run. He left for Salt Lake City with two of his staff members and stayed there for a while. "We stayed at the Salt Lake City Hotel. In one of the bedrooms we laid out the film, using every piece of furniture.... It being against the law to have anything dangerously inflammable in a hotel, we had to go about it secretly.... With such heart-breaking handicaps and without the proper facilities, by some miracle we finished the cutting."[114]

The film's first screening declared that it was an outright success but Charlie still couldn't breathe the free air. Although he shifted to the Ritz Hotel in New York, he was to stay hidden until the process-servers stopped harassing him. In the middle of all this, he suddenly wanted to go to the dinner party of Frank Harris, to which he was invited. "That evening a heavily veiled woman passed through the lobby of the Ritz and got into a taxi – it was me!"[115]

Frank Harris was an author and Charlie loved his books and admired the man. This feeling was mutual as Frank too admired Charlie's works. He admitted this when in August 1919, he had sent him his book, writing a short piece inside, saying that he was "one of the few who has helped me without even knowing me, one whose rare artistry in humour I have often admired, for those who make men laugh are worthier than those who make them weep."[116]

A couple of days later, First National approached Charlie directly, asking him to screen the movie for them. They now seemed like wanting to buy the movie. After the screening was done, J.D. Williams, the president of the company asked Charlie to wait for a while. But Charlie had lost his patience. "After the way they had treated me, I had no respect for them. However, they quickly made up their minds and my lawyer drew up an agreement to the effect that I was to receive fifty per cent of the profits after they had recouped their million and a half."[117] It was time for Charlie to now breathe some fresh and healthy air. His divorce case was over and he was now rid of the lawsuit regarding the movie. He took a little vacation of his own, in New York, not wanting to think of work or anything.

In New York, he was invited to several parties and other such events. He chose to go to a few and it was there that he met Waldo Frank. Waldo was a writer, who had later written an article on Chaplin, which was published in September 1929 by *Scribner's Magazine*. Charlie wrote in his autobiography that this was the first serious article to be ever written about him.

Charlie also met the poet, Hart Crane, who before dying had written a poem, "Chaplinesque", which was dedicated to Charlie.

His Second Marriage and Befriending Hearst

Very little is known about Charlie's second wife, Lita Grey. Charlie himself had mentioned about her in his autobiography only a few times, never ever giving her name. He married Lita secretly in 1924, when she got pregnant with his child. She was only sixteen at that time, and Chaplin married her basically to avoid being a part of a scandal.

Their marriage lasted only three years, ending in a bad divorce in 1927. Together they had two sons, Charles Jr. and Sydney Earl, whom Charlie loved a lot, and he admitted that it was for their sake that he did not write much about their mother in his book.

Lita was supposed to play the lead role in *The Gold Rush*, but due to their personal problems, she was dismissed. Previously, she had played a small part in both, *The Kid* and *The Idle Class*.

It was during this time that Charlie met William R. Hearst. He was an American publisher who owned a chain of newspapers and was one of the pioneers in the journalism business in America. Charlie began visiting his house frequently, probably to avoid going to his own, due to his recent estrangement with Lita. Gradually, Hearst became a very good friend to Charlie and their friendship lasted for a very long time. Hearst was one of the few who had supported Charlie when the rest of the American Press had gone against him during the late 1940s. About him, Charlie had said, "If I were asked what personality in my life has made the deepest impression on me, I would say the late William Randolph Hearst.... It was his shrewdness, his kindness, his ruthlessness, his immense power and wealth, and above all, his genuine naturalness. In worldly values, he was the freest man I have ever known."[118]

❑

A Tale of Two Extraordinary Films

The Gold Rush

"In the creation of comedy, it is paradoxical that tragedy stimulates the spirit of ridicule; because ridicule, I suppose, is an attitude of defiance: we must laugh in the face of our helplessness against the forces of nature – or go insane."[119]

The Gold Rush was one of the most successful feature films of Charlie. Many might not know much about his other films, but this is one of the few that is not just Charlie's best, but also comes under the list of the best silent films ever been made.

Charlie got the idea to make this film after watching some images of Alaska, Klondike and Chilkoot Pass. In some of the images, he saw a line of people climbing up the frozen mountains. He instantly got the idea of making this film, but he still needed a deeper plot.

Then he came across a book which was about how a group of people, who were going to California, got stuck in the snowy mountains of Sierra Nevada. He read that many people died of hunger and the ones who survived had resorted to either cannibalism or roasting their shoes and eating them. "Out of this harrowing tragedy I conceived one of our funniest scenes. In dire hunger, I boil my shoes and eat it, picking the nails as though they were bones of a delicious capon, and eating the shoe-laces as though they were spaghetti. In this delirium of hunger, my partner is convinced I am a chicken and wants to eat me."[120]

"I think that what attracted Chaplin was this sense of remoteness and isolation, the absence of civilized apparatus, and the necessity for creating social life and relationships anew. These ideas are strongly present in his film. They are one thing that makes it possible for the film, while remaining a farcical comedy, to provoke unusually large questions about the significance of life."[121]

Charlie had decided to cast Lita Grey as the leading lady for this film. But as has already been established, they had an affair and she ended up getting pregnant and eventually getting married to him. This led Charlie to search for a new leading lady. Then he saw Georgia Hales in the movie *The Salvation Hunters* and immediately decided to cast her.

David Robinson wrote an article on the filming of the movie, in which he described the shooting in the following words, "It was in every respect the most elaborate undertaking of Chaplin's career. For two weeks, the unit shot on location at Truckee in the snow country of the Sierra Nevada. Here Chaplin faithfully recreated the historic image of the prospectors struggling up the Chilkoot Pass. Six hundred extras, many drawn from the vagrants and derelicts of Sacramento, were brought by train, to clamber up the 2,300-feet pass dug through the mountain snow.

For the main shooting, the unit returned to the Hollywood studio, where a remarkably convincing miniature mountain range was created out of timber (a quarter of a million feet, it was reported), chicken wire, burlap, plaster, salt and flour. The spectacle of this Alaskan snowscape improbably glistening under the baking Californian summer sun drew crowds of sightseers.

In addition, the studio technicians devised exquisite models to produce the special effects which Chaplin demanded, like the miners' hut which is blown by the tempest to teeter on the edge of a precipice, for one of the cinema's most sustained sequences of comic suspense. Often it is impossible to detect the shift from model to full-size set."[122]

When this film was released, it not only covered the losses of the United Artists, but also gave new confidence to the company. Before this, Charlie had only made one movie, and without him, for the past few years, Mary Pickford and Douglas Fairbanks were doing well, but not too great.

There are a number of beautiful scenes in the movie, which together made the experience of the audience a wonderful one.

For instance, the dancing-bun scene, where Charlie, in order to entertain Georgia and her friends, puts a fork in each bun and makes it dance on the table. Although this happens in Charlie's dream, after he falls asleep waiting for his guests, the scene is still remembered today for its uniqueness. "It is a beautiful and memorable scene, but its effect is a matter of poetic suggestiveness rather than any obvious dramatic intention.... Despite the appearance of jollity, a current of sadness and disappointment runs through the scene, deriving not just from the occasion but from all Charlie's doubts and fears about his love relationship. Yet there is no trace of self-pity. When the dance happens, it is photographed close, in a subdued light, without distracting reminders of its fictional audience.

It seems to be addressed directly to us.... Sadness, self-pity and anticipated disappointment are fed into the act, and emerge as self-forgetful absorption. It is one of Chaplin's subtlest creations, and takes the comedy of feeling as far as it will go."[123]

The scene where Charlie eats his own shoe after boiling it has special mention by anyone who attempts to review the film. As has already been mentioned, it is one of the funniest scenes in the film. "If the random hostilities of the cabin ménage count as defeats for Charlie, the boot-eating is his victory. It shows that, as well as his cunning, Charlie brings his courtesy to the wild. His courtesy is a manifestation of display: represented here by his addiction to the conventions of gourmet dining, it is his reaction to the dehumanizing menace of hunger, a polite but firm contradiction of the indifferent brutality of the wild.... In its comic effects, the scene is complex. It is full of suggestiveness and surprise. At its heart is the obvious incongruity between the unappetizing boot and the Savoy Grill delicacy with which it is prepared. But Charlie is not content with a single joke. He must elaborate and improvise. So, in his hands, the dumb boot undergoes a series of swift transformations, as the laces become spaghetti, the ruptured sole a Dover sole, and a bent nail a wishbone.... Another element of the humorous effect is provided by the act of consumption, in the contrast between Charlie's encouraging display of satisfaction and Jim's glum disbelief in the nourishing properties of the face. The boot-eating, in fact, marks a stage in the relationship between Charlie and Jim, which is itself important in the film."[124]

In the end, when Charlie and Jim become millionaires after digging gold, they buy first-class tickets to go back home. The press is also after them to publish their story and click their pictures. Although it looks a bit too fantastic, Charlie seems to be quite at ease with this new found wealth. He then finds Georgia, who is sitting by herself looking gloomy, and invites her to join him. The last shot is of the photographer clicking a picture of Charlie, while he kisses Georgia.

"*The Gold Rush* is in many respects a paean of praise to the manifold pleasures of money, food, drink, love and conviviality. It is from the tension between the two kinds of value dramatized in the film – material and non-material – that Charlie derives his adaptability and resilience. His answer to the film's looming question can be said to read, you can live on old boots if you have to, but should enjoy the good things in life when you can. It may sound an obvious recipe, but it is harder, and wiser, than it seems."[125]

The movie was released in August 1925, and was an instant hit; and when Charlie attended its premiere, he observed that almost every scene had received a good laugh, followed by applause. It was one of the highest grossing silent films ever made.

The Circus

"*The Circus* won Charles Chaplin his first Academy Award – it was still not yet called the *Oscar* – he was given it at the first presentation ceremony, in 1929. The special award was for *Versatility and Genius in Writing, Acting, Directing and Producing.*"[126]

Charlie had a tough time during the making of *The Circus.* It was the period when he was going through his divorce with Lita Grey, his second wife. This case had become such a sensation throughout the country that all sorts of bad stories were being published about Charlie in the papers. This made it difficult for him to concentrate and the lawsuit itself delayed the movie's production, wherein he had to stop working for about eight months. The lawyers then tried to seize his studio, which led Charlie to sneak out with whatever materials he required for the film.

But this was the least of the problems which Charlie faced. The worst soon followed. "Even before shooting began, the huge circus tent, which provides the principal setting for the film, was destroyed by gales. After four weeks of filming, Chaplin discovered that bad laboratory work had made everything already shot unusable. In the ninth month of shooting, a fire raged through the studio, destroying sets and props. Later, when the unit returned to work after the enforced lay-off, they found that Hollywood's mushroom real-estate development had in the meantime transformed the scenery beyond recognition. The troubles persisted to the very end. For the final scene, of the Circus moving out of town, the wagons were towed to location. When the unit returned for the second day's shooting, the whole circus train had vanished. It had been stolen by some high-spirited students, who planned to use it for a marathon bonfire. This time, luckily, Chaplin was just in time to prevent the catastrophe. Somehow, from all the chaos, Chaplin conjured a film of deft comedy and admirable structure."[127]

Probably, it was the pain of going through his divorce and the problems during its making that Charlie manages to exclude the mention of this film or its making in his autobiography. It seemed as if the entire episode had just been wiped out from his memory.

Charlie ended up making this movie after having one thought of a particular gag. It was the scene where he is walking on a tight-rope and a group of monkeys strip him off his clothes. Then he built the whole film around it.

The Circus is one of Charlie's only movies where

he plays a part of a man who is in love with a girl, but when he sees that she is not, he helps her to get back with her love. He takes on the role of a mediator in another couple's love story, being a true fool, pathetic and miserable, but still not letting the audience pity him as he swings his cane and struts like a penguin into the open field that had housed the circus a few days back.

This time Charlie also had a control on his emotions. His tramp did not go overboard with expressions and acted much like a sensible man, who seemed to know what he was doing. There are a few scenes in this movie that are particularly remembered even today for its refreshing honesty.

The scene where Charlie is being chased by the police, after they mistake him to be a thief, is one of the highlights of the movie. "It is a virtuoso Chaplin opening: hectic in pace, rich in incident, full of suspense and surprise. It also establishes, wittily and economically, the themes of the film.... Charlie's disorienting trials in the purgatory of the fairground continue in the maze of mirrors, where he is driven by the cop, and where, suddenly confronted with multiple images of himself, he has trouble sorting out the true from the false.... His resourcefulness is carried over to the next episode, when the pursuit leads to a carnival tableau of Noah's Ark dummies. Charlie evades capture by smartly taking the place of a retired automation, and swivelling on the spot with gestures of paralytic precision.... Finally, he is chased into the circus ring, where he tangles involuntarily with the magician's act, in an amusing piece of drama confusion."[128]

The second most remembered scene of the movie is when Charlie walks on the tight-rope. The fact that he actually learns the act is in itself spectacular. "The tight-rope act is the culmination of Charlie's performing career, and the climax of the film. It is one of Chaplin's great balancing act finales." In the movie, Charlie asks one of the circus technicians to handle his safety harness, as he really doesn't know how to walk on the rope. He only does the act because of his love for Merna and because he has been asked to perform a successful act or else he would be fired. In the middle of the act, his harness breaks loose while he is still walking on the rope unaided. "Irony is provided by his temporary unawareness of the defection of the harness (rendering his confident shimmies on the rope much more audacious than he supposes), and suspense is augmented by his invariable talent for complication, resulting in the released swarm of monkeys that attach themselves to his face and divest him of his trousers."[129]

Charlie eventually manages to get off the rope, completing the act by riding on the bicycle and out of the circus. The last scene has Charlie deciding to give away Merna to the man she really loves. This self-sacrificing act, if not anything else, only goes on to show how Charlie has grown over the years.

The Circus, released in January 1928, wasn't his best movie, but certainly was one of his good movies which even won him an award.

Charlie is not just remembered for his most popular movies, but also for the little wonderful acts from his many other less-liked movies, which bring out the whole in him. This, of course, does not mean that *The Circus* was at all trivial; in fact, it was a brilliant movie, in the sense that it brought out the character of the tramp to its fullest extent. In the end, it doesn't even matter if there was not a single mention of it in his autobiography.

❑

The Life of a Celebrity

As and when a person becomes a world phenomenon, his ideas and opinions begin to be taken seriously, and then every other prominent personality expresses their desire to meet them.

Something like this also happened with Charlie Chaplin. In no time, Charlie was getting his head sculpted, being quoted by various magazines and papers, and meeting some significant others, who had changed the way the world worked.

The sculptress who carved the bust of Charlie was Clare Sheridan. Her claim to fame was her book *From Mayfair to Moscow*. When she came to Hollywood, Charlie was obliged to meet her. She then suggested that she would like to sculpt his head. "So arrangements were made to bring her clay and tools to my house, and after lunch I would sit for her into the late afternoon.... Near the completion of the bust, I examined it. 'This could be the head of a criminal,' I said. 'On the contrary,' she answered with mock solemnity, 'it's the head of a genius.' I laughed and developed a theory about the genius and the criminal being closely allied, both being extreme individualists."[130]

When had Charlie transformed into this beautiful philosopher, no one knows. But one thing can be said, that it was probably the result of all his struggles when he was just a child.

Charlie never once thought of his life to be meaningless. He always wore a face of confidence and purpose and thought life to be as beautiful as it could get. All this, he could still feel only because of his upbringing, as he once said that his mother taught him and Sydney never to feel small and always treated them as special, no matter how deprived they were.

Charlie's own words verify his philosophy on the importance of life. "I cannot believe that our existence is meaningless or accidental, as some scientists would tell us. Life or death are too resolute, too implacable to be accidental. The ways of life and death – genius cut down in its prime, world upheavals, holocausts and catastrophes – may seem futile and meaningless. But the fact that these things have happened are demonstrable of a resolute, fixed purpose beyond the comprehension of our three-dimensional minds."[131]

Charlie also wrote in his autobiography, about what religion meant to him. "I am not religious in the dogmatic sense.... I neither believe nor disbelieve in anything. That which can be imagined is as much an approximation to truth as that which can be proved by mathematics."[132]

He also explained his theory on faith in the unknown. He really believed that faith was much more powerful than it was given credit for and that, without it, people wouldn't have been able to create anything. "As I grow older, I am becoming more preoccupied with faith.... I believe that faith is a precursor of all our ideas. Without faith, there never could have evolved hypothesis, theory, science or mathematics. I believe that faith is an extension of the mind. It is the key that negates the impossible. To deny faith is to refute oneself and the spirit that generates all our creative forces. My faith is in the unknown, in all that we do not understand by reason; I believe that what is beyond our comprehension is a simple fact in other dimensions, and that, in the realm of the unknown, there is an infinite power for good."[133]

Charlie first met Einstein when the latter had come to America in 1926 for a lecture. "I have a theory that scientists and philosophers are sublimated romanticists, who channel their passions in another direction. This theory fitted well the personality of Einstein."[134]

During a dinner conversation, Mrs. Einstein told Charlie the story of how her husband came up with his theory of relativity. "The Doctor came down in his dressing-gown as usual for breakfast but he hardly touched a thing. I thought something was wrong, so I asked what was troubling him. 'Darling,' he said, 'I have a wonderful idea.' And after drinking his coffee, he went to the piano and started playing. Now and again he would stop, making a few notes then repeat: 'I've got a wonderful idea, a marvellous idea!' I said, 'Then for goodness' sake, tell me what it is, don't keep me in suspense.' He said: "It's difficult, I still have to work it out.' She told me he continued playing the piano and making notes for about half an hour, then went upstairs to his study, telling her that he did not wish to be disturbed, and remained there for two weeks. 'Each day I sent him up his meals,' she said, 'and in the evening, he would walk a little for exercise, then return to his work.' 'Eventually,' she said, 'he came down from his study looking very pale.' 'That's it', he told me, wearily putting two sheets of paper on the table. And that was his theory of relativity."[135]

Einstein came back to America, when the Second World War began and decided that he would not return to Germany, as he did not believe in the policies of the Nazi Party. Here, he joined the Princeton University as a Professor in order to pursue a better life.

Charlie also got to meet Sergei Eisenstein, the director of the famous *Battleship Potemkin.* From him, Charlie learnt new techniques and the importance of portraying history on the screen. "After all, there are more valid facts and details in works of art than there are in history books."[136]

Life was such that Charlie was needed everywhere, but he chose to meet only a few, the ones whom he really regarded as significant. In his autobiography, these are a few pictures of him being photographed with some such personalities. Among them were Winston Churchill, Albert Einstein with his wife, Lord and Lady Mountbatten and Arnold Schoenberg.

❑

Arrival of the Talkies and Charlie's Revolt

The synchronization of sound in films had recently been devised and Charlie was told that it would soon revolutionize the entire film industry. He did not want to believe it. And he certainly did not want to join the revolution either.

Then he saw the first sound film produced by Warner Brothers, and it made him even more determined about his theories. He described the movie in the following words, "It was a costume picture, showing a very lovely actress – who shall be nameless – emoting silently over some great sorrow, her big soulful eyes imparting anguish beyond the eloquence of Shakespeare. Then suddenly a new element entered the film – the noise that one hears when putting sea-shell to one's ear. Then the lovely princess spoke as if talking through sand: 'I shall marry Gregory, even at the cost of giving up the throne.' It was a terrible shock, for until then the princess had enthralled us. As the picture progressed, the dialogue became funnier, but not as funny as the sound effects. When the handle of the boudoir door turned, I thought someone had cracked up a farm tractor, and when the door closed, it sounded like the collision of two lumber trucks... I came away from the theatre believing the days of sound were numbered."[137]

Talkies became the new trend only after MGM produced *The Broadway Melody*, which was a sound musical. "That started it; overnight every theatre began wiring for sound. That was the twilight of silent films."[138]

Tim Dirks, a renowned film critic wrote in his essay about how the talkies took over the film industry. "Silent film studios became obsolescent, and new investments had to be made for expensive new equipment, technological innovations, and sound-proofed stages. Cameras were mounted on moveable, squeak-proofed dollies, and microphones were hung from booms that could be held above the action (outside of the camera's view).... Films that began production as silents were quickly transformed into sound films. All of the studios were forced to follow suit. By 1930, the silent movie had practically disappeared, and by the mid-1930s, film industry studios had become sound-film factories."[139]

Charlie's *City Lights* appeared in theatres in February 1931. Why did he choose to still make a silent film? Charlie says that it was because he was a pantomime artist and believed in the uniqueness of this art form.

David Robinson, in his article, explained further why Charlie was adamant to make yet another silent movie. "Even before he began *City Lights*, the sound film was firmly established. This new revolution was a bigger challenge to Chaplin than to other silent stars. His Tramp character was universal. His mime was understood in every part of the world. But if the Tramp now began to speak in English, that world-wide audience would instantly shrink. Moreover, there was the problem of how he should talk. Everyone, across the world, had formed his or her own fantasy of the Tramp's voice. How could he now impose a single, monolingual voice?"[140]

There are two main themes in the movie. The main subject of the film is the leading lady's blindness. Charlie had previously thought of having a circus clown who turns blind after an accident, but it did not match with the rest of the story. Then he decided to have the leading lady play the role of a blind flower girl. She and the tramp have a fairy-tale love-affair until she gets her sight back.

The scene, in which the tramp and the flower girl, played by Virginia Cherrill, meet for the first time, is much talked about. "He spent many laborious weeks on the deceptively simple scene where the Tramp and the flower girl first meet, setting up the premise of the story. Here, in two or three minutes, through action alone, he establishes the meeting of the two people: the Tramp's recognition that she is blind, and his instant fascination and pity and the girl's misconception that this poor creature is a rich man. At the end of the sequence, having built up the sentiment to a high pitch, he brilliantly dashes it with a touch of broad comedy."[141]

It was one of the most difficult scenes which Charlie had to direct. The shot is about a little more than one minute long, but it took him five days to get it completely right. "This was not the girl's fault, but partly my own, for I had worked myself into a neurotic state of wanting perfection."[142]

The second theme of the movie involves a drunken rich man, played by Harry Myers, who is shown as depressed and suicidal. "The first thing to notice about Harry is that he is, in his comical way, a 'tragic' figure.... We first meet him in the act of trying to drown himself, and he introduces into the film a note of suicidal despair that threatens Charlie's safety as well as his own. He doesn't have Charlie's protection against the painfulness of his feelings, and can only take refuge from them in drink."[143]

When the tramp saves his life, he feels indebted to him and takes him to his house and treats him like a friend. But the problem arises after he wakes up the next morning and doesn't remember the tramp or anything that happened with him last night.

One of the main highlights of the movie is its opening scene, which has a deeper meaning attached to it. It is the scene where a statue is being unveiled and Charlie is found sleeping on it. "What is satirised here is simply social pretension, the studied denial of inconvenient feeling. This is the dominant habit of the top-hatted types who attend the unveiling: represented by the pompous monumentality of the statues they have come to see, which Charlie, planting his bum upon one outstretched hand and converting the solemn statue of another into a cocked snook, endows with a suddenly ribald life. Charlie's function is to introduce some human crudity into the dignified proceedings: he represents the class of feelings which the high society pretends to ignore."[144]

Charlie gave his own music to the film, as he "wanted the music to be a counterpoint of grace and charm, to express sentiment"[145] but the music arrangers did not understand this. After the synchronization of music and video was done, Charlie tried experimenting with the audience. He screened the movie without any announcements. As was feared, not many turned up, and those who did, left the movie without it being finished. At first Charlie thought that it was because the audience had moved on to talkies. Then a thought came to him that probably it was because he had not yet tried to sell the film. Little did he know that this selling would also become a problem for him. "In the past, exhibitors had always had a lively interest in a new film of mine; now their interest was only lukewarm. Moreover, difficulties arose about getting a New York showing. All the New York movie houses were booked up I was told. So I would have to wait my turn."[146]

While Charlie was working out ways and means to sell the rights in New York, Alf Reeves got them a deal to screen his movie in a theatre in Los Angeles. At the premiere, when the opening scene received a tremendous laughter, Charlie realised that all the hard work had paid out. Dr. Einstein and his wife had also accompanied Charlie, and in the end, the Doctor was found with tears in his eyes. "During the final scene, I noticed Einstein wiping his eyes – further evidence that scientists are incurable sentimentalists."[147]

Second Europe Visit

Then Charlie decided to go to London and launch the film there. This was one of the biggest moments in his life, as he was now returning to his motherland, as the most successful moviemaker in Hollywood.

This time Charlie met a whole lot of new people, the ones which he had missed the last time he was here. George Bernard Shaw was amongst them.

Charlie admitted that he was a little embarrassed when he visited Shaw's library. He was invited by Shaw to his house along with some other guests. "Afterwards, G.B. took me into his library – just the two of us.... The library was a bright cheerful room that looked out on the Thames. And, lo and behold, I found myself confronted with a shelf of Shaw's books over the mantelpiece, and like a fool, having read very little of Shaw, I went over them with an exclamation of 'Ah, all your works!' Then it occurred to me that he might have brought about this opportune moment to explore my mind through discussing his books.... How I should have liked this to happen. But instead there was a mincing moment of silence as I smiled and turned away and looked about the room and made some banal comment on its cheerfulness."[148]

Charlie also met Winston Churchill in England, although he had met him before, when the latter had come to America. That time, they had talked about the condition of England for a very long time, and Churchill started showing his interest, the moment Charlie spoke about the Labour Government.

In England, Churchill invited Charlie to Chartwell, which was an old house that Churchill had built for his family. After spending more time with Churchill, Charlie was much impressed by him. He wrote in his autobiography, "Sir Winston, I should imagine, has had more fun than most of us. On the stage of life, he has played many parts with courage, zest and a remarkable enthusiasm. He has missed very few pleasures in this world.... He has enjoyed power but has never been obsessed by it. In his busy life, he has found time for hobbies: brick-laying, horse-racing and painting."[149]

During this time, Mahatma Gandhi also came to London and Charlie expressed his desire to meet him. He did not know much about Gandhi, except that he was "the symbol of what the Indian people want"[150] and that he went on hunger strikes and boycott of foreign goods in order to achieve independence. If Charlie had any thoughts or opinions regarding the British Raj in India, he showed none.

When Charlie met Gandhi, he asked him about his thoughts on machinery. Charlie wanted to know as to why this man was so against the use of machinery, which incidentally had helped their own country so much in its development.

"The Mahatma nodded and smiled as I continued: 'After all, if machinery is used in the altruistic sense, it should help to release man from the bondage of slavery, and give him shorter hours of labour and time to improve his mind and enjoy life.'

'I understand,' he said, speaking calmly, 'but before India can achieve those aims, she must first rid herself of English rule. Machinery in the past has made us dependent on England, and the only way we can rid ourselves of that dependence is to boycott all goods made by machinery.... That is our form of attaching a very powerful nation like England – and, of course, there are other reasons.'"[151]

Charlie was not disappointed with the answers that he received from Gandhi; in fact, he was much amazed. "I got a lucid object lesson in tactical manoeuvring in India's fight for freedom, inspired, paradoxically, by a realistic, virile-minded visionary with a will of iron to carry it out. He also told me that supreme independence is to shed oneself of unnecessary things, and that violence eventually destroys itself."[152]

Much had changed since Charlie's last visit to London. He could now see no old ladies sleeping by the Thames Embankment. The poverty which had previously stared at them was gone. He also saw well-fed children running about in the streets. England was coming out of its destitution and Charlie could not help but feel a sense of happiness, although he had nothing to do with it.

H.G. Wells had now taken an apartment in Baker Street, and while Charlie was still in London, he visited him quite often. They had become quite close and Charlie mainly talked about politics with him. His interest in socialism made Wells once ask him about it.

Charlie replied, "It was not until I came to the United States and met Upton Sinclair... he asked me in his soft-spoken way if I believed in the profit system. I said facetiously that it required an accountant to answer that. It was a disarming question, but instinctively I felt it went to the very root of the matter, and from that moment, I became interested and saw politics not as history but as an economic problem."[153]

Then Charlie decided to go to France. He came to know that his brother, Sydney had now retired from work and was living in a small but comfortable house with his wife in Nice, which was a city located on the south-east coast of France.

It had been a long time since he had met his brother, but before heading for Nice, he wanted to visit Paris. He stayed there for around two days and then moved on to Folies Bergère, where he met with Alfred Jackson, who had been his friend and colleague during his association with the Eight Lancashire Lads.

Charlie, in his autobiography, also shared an interesting story about how he was once tricked into answering questions about war and then was misquoted in a newspaper article. It happened during this particular visit. "I happened to be waiting on the tennis court for my partner, when a young gentleman introduced himself as a friend of a friend of mine. After an exchange of mutual pleasantries, we drifted on to mutual subjects.... I talked on many subjects. On the state of world affairs, I wallowed pessimistically, telling him that the situation in Europe was leading up to another war.... We parted in a cordial way. I believe I made a date the next evening, but he never showed up. And lo! Instead of talking to a friend, I discovered I had been talking to a news reporter; and the next day, a front-page spread was in the newspapers: 'Charlie Chaplin no patriot!'"[154]

Charlie's patriotism was of a different kind. He did not believe that war was the solution to the problems of the world. And he certainly did not wish to die in its name. "I cannot vociferate about national pride.... Naturally, if the country in which I lived were to be invaded, like most of us, I believe I would be capable of an act of supreme sacrifice. But I am incapable of a fervent love of homeland, for it has only to turn Nazi and I would leave it without compunction – and from what I have observed, the cells of Nazism, although dormant at the moment, can be activated very quickly in every country. Therefore, I do not wish to make any sacrifice for a political cause unless I personally believe in it. I am no martyr for nationalism – neither do I wish to die for a president, a prime minister or a dictator."[155]

Charlie next went to Berlin unaware about the bad stories which were being published against him by the Nazi Press. He had a good time there, owing to the fact that he did not read any of those articles. Once here, Charlie was also very eager to meet Einstein again; so one evening he dropped by their apartment and dined with them.

It seemed that Charlie was whiling away his time in Europe and did not wish to go back. It was true. Since sound films had become so popular, he could not understand what to do about it. He wanted to remain loyal to his medium, but he was also aware of the harsh reality that the silent era was over. "Occasionally I mused over the possibility of making a sound film, but the thought sickened me, for I realised I could never achieve the excellence of my silent pictures. It would mean giving up my tramp character entirely. Some people suggested that the tramp might talk. This was unthinkable, for the first word that he ever uttered would transform him into another person. Besides, the matrix out of which he was born was as mute as the rags he wore."[156]

Charlie spent some more time in Europe, going back to Paris and then to London. This time, he met the Prince of Wales and also visited the house of Shakespeare which is situated in Stratford.

Now Charlie decided that he should go back and start a new project. But while he was preparing to return to California, he suddenly received a telegram from his friend, Fairbanks, who asked him to come to St. Moritz.

He was too happy to see him and even called upon Sydney to join them. Fairbanks, it seemed, had also been worried about his future in the film industry, as all he knew was how to mime. Together, they tried to forget about all their worries and just enjoy the mountains of Switzerland, indulging in the wonderful sport of skiing.

A Short Visit to Japan

Since Charlie was in no hurry to return to America, he decided to reach California taking the Eastern route while stopping in Japan for a few days. Sydney too agreed to join him but only till Japan.

They sailed through Alexandria in Egypt and then through the Red Sea and reached the port of Singapore. Here they stopped for a while and saw some Chinese plays. Although Charlie could not understand their language, he felt the emotions fully.

Their next stop was Bali. Sydney had suggested that they should stay in Bali for some time, as he had heard that it was called a paradise. And it did turn out to be a wonderful experience. They visited the city in its raw stage, when there was no education, no industry and no development. "Natives worked four months in the rice-fields and devoted the other eight months to art and culture. Entertainment was free all over the island, one village performing for the other."[157]

Sydney and Charlie entered Japan as the guests of the government. They reached the Kobe harbour and saw that a crowd had gathered there to greet them. "The sight of numerous brightly coloured kimonos against the background of smoke-stacks and the drab grey docks was paradoxically beautiful."[158]

Charlie was unaware about the impending dangers that were lurking in the streets of Japan. When they were on their way to the hotel, Kono, their Japanese secretary asked them to get down of the car and bow towards the palace and said that it was customary. "This request somewhat bewildered me, because no one was around except the two or three cars that had followed us. If it were customary, the public would have known and a crowd would have been there, if only a small one."[159]

As and when the day progressed, Sydney started suspecting that something was wrong. But Charlie still thought that it was nothing. Next day, in their hotel room, Sydney discovered that their bags had been thoroughly scrutinized and that all their documents had been touched by someone else.

It was only when Charlie received another strange request from Kono that he realised that something was seriously odd about their visit. He was asked to meet a merchant, who wanted to show them some pictures. This seemed very weird to him. When he refused to meet such a man, Kono tried insisting, but Charlie was adamant.

Then the next day, a few young men came to them while they were having dinner. When Kono's expression changed and he looked concerned, Charlie lost his nerve and asked the men who they were. "Kono, without looking up from his plate, mumbled: 'He says you've insulted his ancestors by refusing to see his pictures.'"[160]

Worried, Charlie asked Kono to call for a taxi and they immediately left the place.

Kono wouldn't explain anything and Charlie did not understand what was happening. On the day when the Prime Minister's son invited him and Sydney to a Sumo wrestling match, the whole scenario became clear to them.

In the middle of the match, the Prime Minister's son received the news of his father, Inukai Tsuyoshi's assassination.[161] It was the work of a few naval officers, accompanied by some army cadets, who came to the house of the Prime Minister and killed him in broad daylight. Their original plan had included something more.

"It was not until Hugh Byas had written his most interesting and informative book *Government by Assassination*, published by Alfred A. Knopf, that the whole mystery, as far as I was involved, was clarified. It appears that the society called The Black Dragon was active at that moment, and it was they who had demanded that I bow to the palace."[162]

Further Charlie quoted from the said book, which had a detailed account of the trial of the Prime Minister's assassins. "Lieutenant Seishi Koga, naval ringleader of the plot, afterwards told the court martial that the conspirators had discussed a plan to bring about martial law by bombing the House of Representatives.... Another plan, which might be too grotesque for credence if it had not been told in court, proposed the killing of Charles Chaplin, then visiting Japan....

Judge: What was the significance of killing Chaplin?

Koga: Chaplin is a popular figure in United States and the darling of the capitalist class. We believed that killing him would cause a war with America, and, thus, we could kill two birds with a single stone."[163]

When Charlie first read about it, he couldn't stop reflecting on its consequences, as for one thing, the assassins had mistaken him to be an American. Whether a war would have taken place between Japan and America or any other country, for that matter, if the plan was carried out successfully, cannot be ascertained, but what can be, is the fact that the world would have certainly missed hearing the voice of Charlie Chaplin, while he sang nonsensically in *Modern Times* (1936) or gave his moving speech in *The Great Dictator* (1940).

❑

The Last of the Tramp

Eight months had passed since Charlie had left for England to launch *City Lights* and now when he returned after visiting several other countries, he still was in a dilemma regarding his future in the movie industry. Though he had known this from before, he was fully convinced now that the sound features are here to stay.

He wandered about in the streets of Hollywood, thinking to himself, whether he should just sell everything and settle in China. Only he knows why he thought of living in China, but the fact that he actually considered retiring, was scary.

Charlie spent some more time trying to adjust to the fact that the time for silent movies had come to an end. He was not getting any fresh ideas and he could not even think of making a talking picture. So he passed his time by meeting people and talking about the issues of the country.

It was 1933, and Franklin D. Roosevelt had come to power. The condition of America was becoming worse and people were becoming cynical. Then Mr. Roosevelt did something which changed the face of the country forever and for good. "That was a moment when America was at its best. Shops and stores of all kinds continued to do business on credit, even the cinemas sold tickets on credit, and for ten days, while Roosevelt and his so-called brains trust formulated the New Deal,[164] the people acted magnificently.... It was inspiring to see how quickly the American citizen reacted to constructive government."[165]

The idea for making *Modern Times* came suddenly to Charlie when he was being interviewed by a news reporter. "Hearing that I was visiting Detroit, hc had told me of the factory-belt system there – a harrowing story of big industry luring healthy young men off the farms who, after four or five years at the belt system, became nervous wrecks."[166]

Charlie used this idea and made a semi-silent film, keeping the tramp and all the other characters, still on mute. The voice, which the movie had, cleverly had its source in other mediums. For instance, when the factory owner is speaking, his voice is booming through a video monitor, which has been installed in several areas inside the factory. It gives him the authority at once, which the audience too recognizes instantly. The second type of voice comes in the form of an instruction manual which is being heard through a tape player.

And then there is the song; Charlie's song. It has no language, which easily makes it universally appealing. It comes almost during the end of the movie, where he is a waiter in a fancy restaurant and has to sing in order to get the permanent job. He keeps forgetting the lyrics, so, Paulette, the leading lady and his love interest in the movie, writes the song in the cuff of his shirt. While dancing, the cuff comes out and, hence, Charlie in a hurry sings this song titled 'Titine' which makes absolutely no sense as it contains a series of words, put together having no meaning at all.

Titine
Se Bella Giu Satore
Je Notre So Cafore
Je Notre Si Cavore
Je La Tu La Ti La Twah
La Spinash O La Bouchon
Cigaretto Portobello
Si Rakish Spaghaletto
Ti La Tu La Ti La Twah
Senora Pilasina
Voulez-Vous Le Taximeter?
Le Zionta Su La Seata
Tu La Tu La Tu La Wa[167]

"His nonsense gives the song a sharper and weirder life than any sense could do. But it is a bit like turning on the radio for a vital announcement and getting an earful of static. The laugh is on us. The conclusion is irresistible that the song is Charlie speaking directly to us, in a calculated act of defiance. It is his answer to the clamour for speech, a demonstration that we can't presume to possess him, but that he remains in the end, as ever, elusive."[168]

Modern Times, as the name suggests, is a movie having the aspects of modernism as its basic theme. It is about how in the wake of industrialisation, it affects the factory workers, who were previously traditional farmers. "*Modern Times* announces itself as 'a story of industry, of individual enterprise – humanity crusading in the pursuit of happiness.'... Charlie finds himself deposited in a different kind of wilderness: a vast, anonymous, modern industrial state, where he is stunted from place to place – factory, jail, store, swamp – in his search for security."[169]

Charlie uses a 'feeding machine' in one of the sequences of this movie, where he is seen as being the victim of yet another machine. In the movie, it is indicated as a time-saving device, in order to make the workers continue working, even during their lunch time. The idea of using such a machine had come to him a long time back. He admits in his autobiography, "As far back as 1916, I had many ideas for feature pictures. One was a trip to the moon, a comic spectacle showing the Olympic Games there and the possibilities of playing about with the laws of gravity. It would have been a satire on progress. I thought of a feeding machine, and also a radio-electric hat that could register one's thoughts; and the trouble I get into when I put it on my head and am introduced to the moon-man's sexy wife. The feeding machine I eventually used in *Modern Times*."[170]

During the making of the movie, Charlie had thought of including normal dialogues, but after a day or two, he decided to completely remove them. It was mainly because he could not understand how to make the tramp speak. There had been so many expectations from the audience and the film critics that he ultimately had to choose not to speak. That's why the only words that the tramp ever speaks are gibberish, and there too, he is singing, smartly avoiding any form of dialogue.

The ending of the movie, as is common to almost all other Chaplin movies, portrays a melancholic exuberance. The couple end up having no home, as they had started, but now with an increased sense of confidence. "'We'll get along', says a title; and the couple, arm in arm, set bravely off down a country lane, towards the horizon."[171]

The movie went well with the audience, although some critics argued that it represented the idea of Communism. "However, the liberal reviewers wrote that it was neither for nor against communism and that metaphorically I had sat on the fence."[172]

Now it was about time that Charlie gave up his character of the tramp. The tramp had to die, for Charlie to be able to speak. And Charlie had to speak, because there was no other option left for him, unless he decided to retire, like most of the other silent movie actors had already done.

❑

A Few Affairs and a Marriage

Before the filming of *Modern Times* had begun, Charlie quietly got married to Paulette Goddard. She was his third wife but not the last one.

Charlie first met Paulette on a yacht, on which he was invited by Joe Schenck. "Joe usually embarked with a bevy of pretty girls, and being desperately lonely, I hoped I might find a pretty little ray of sunlight."[173]

Paulette was a divorcee and was trying to invest a part of her alimony, into a film project. Charlie got to know about it while having a conversation with her, following which he tried to advise her to not go for this investment. Eventually, she agreed and that was when they became good friends.

"The bond between Paulette and me was loneliness. She was just out from New York and knew no one. It was a case of Robinson Crusoe discovering Friday for both of us."[174]

Paulette was an actress and soon she began working for a Samuel Goldwyn[175] movie. And Charlie was still wandering around, thinking of what to do with his future. Their relationship developed and shortly they started being seen together everywhere.

Charlie and Paulette sometimes went to look at boats on the San Pedro harbour. Once Paulette commented that if they had such a boat, she would have loved to spend her Sundays on it and visit Catalina. That was all that was necessary for Charlie to hear.

One day, he brought her to the harbour and told her that the owner of one of their favourite boats had invited them to have breakfast. But when she entered the boat, she found that the chefs who had cooked for them were Charlie's and then Charlie told her that he had finally bought the boat. Together they went for a short trip to Catalina for a few days.

One of the reasons for Charlie's inspiration to make *Modern Times* has already been given; the other reason was Paulette Goddard. "Paulette and I went to Tijuana race-track in Mexico, where the winner of the Kentucky something or other was to be presented with a silver cup. Paulette was asked if she could present the cup to the winning jockey and say a few words with a Southern accent.... I was astonished to hear her over the loudspeaker.... This convinced me that she could act. Thus, I was stimulated."[176]

Suddenly, Charlie decided to go to China. It was after the movie was released. He just wanted to go as far away as possible from everything for a while. He and Paulette had just arrived in San Francisco and while they were passing by some warehouses, Charlie saw the name 'China' written on some of the boxes; hence this impulsive decision.

They first arrived in Tokyo, where Charlie had purposely used a false name for registration, as he did not want to be recognized. Nonetheless, when the officials saw his passport, he could not be hidden anymore. In Japan, the government officials never left his side, thus, making his stay a rather dull one.

In Hong Kong, they spent about five months, during which time, they got married. Some had expressed their doubt about whether they were actually married, but all their misgivings were resolved after Charlie announced in public about Paulette being his third wife. Their marriage lasted for six years, and when it finally ended in June 1942, Paulette did not create any drama, like the previous two wives of Charlie had done. Nevertheless, the divorce did bring sadness to Charlie. "The wrench naturally hurt, for it was hard cleaving eight years' association for one's life."[177]

While they were still married, Paulette also acted in *The Great Dictator*, which incidentally was the first talking picture of Charlie. She was a special girl in Charlie's life, as she was the only one who left him on friendlier terms. "She was something of a match for Chaplin – strong willed, independent, a lover of life – her very personality an influence itself on the characters Charlie wrote for her in her two Chaplin films."[178]

The Affairs

In between his marriages, Charlie also had had quite a number of affairs. One was with Pola Negri, a Polish actress, who had initially helped him to get along when he was in Germany for the first time.

When Pola met Charlie the next time, at a symphony concert at Hollywood Bowl, she practically threw herself at him. She kept complaining about why he never called her and that she had come to Hollywood, just to meet him; while Charlie stood there bewildered as to why he would have kept in touch with her anyway. After all, they weren't even good friends then.

"I was sceptical about all this ardour, but attention from the beautiful Pola had its effect on me. A few days later, I was invited to a party she gave at her rented house in Beverly Hills.... This was the beginning of our exotic relationship."[179]

Such was their bond that some papers even published rumours about their engagement. This upset Pola so much that she asked Charlie to issue a statement saying that it was not true. But Charlie was adamant and said that she should be the one doing it.

Next day, Charlie received a call from Pola's maid, who said that she had fallen ill. It turned out to be nothing. Then a few days later, Charlie Hayton, the manager of Paramount studios came to meet Charlie regarding the matter. "It was almost midnight when he arrived.... 'Charlie, all these rumours in the Press is making Pola ill. Why don't you make a statement and stop them?'

Confronted in such a blatant manner, I looked at him squarely. 'What do you want me to say?'

With humorous audacity, he tried to hide his embarrassment. 'You're fond of her, aren't you?'

'I don't think that's anyone's business,' I answered.

'But we have millions invested in this woman! And this publicity is bad for her.' He paused. 'Charlie, if you're fond of her, why don't you marry her?'

At that moment, I saw little humour in this incredible affront. 'If you think I am going to marry someone just to safeguard Paramount's investment, you're very much mistaken'.... And as suddenly as my relationship with Pola had begun, so it ended. She never called me again."[180]

The relationship with Pola had not been half as crazy as the one with a woman, whom Charlie never named in his autobiography.

He met this woman on his second trip to Europe, after the release of *City Lights*. He was in France, passing his time in Côte d' Azur, where he saw her. "She was footloose like myself and we accepted each other at face value.... Our relationship, though not discussed, was understood; she knew that eventually I would return to America."[181]

But gradually Charlie realised that he started having feelings for her, so much so that he could not even think of leaving her behind. Then one day, they were at a casino where she saw her former lover. After they left, she asked Charlie to go back to the hotel, and that she will come in a while. When she did not return after a couple of hours, Charlie understood that she was with him.

When she returned, Charlie confronted her about her former lover but she denied having met him. That was the end of their relationship as after that incident, Charlie completely lost interest in her, while she kept begging him to take her back.

Even though Charlie had nothing to do with her anymore, the story did not end here. She managed to get on board with him on their way to Paris. Throughout the journey, they did not speak to each other but the next day, in Paris, she asked Charlie to have lunch with her. Charlie had politely refused but when he came down to the lobby with another friend, he found that she was waiting for him. Cornered, Charlie could do nothing except to take her along for lunch.

He then left her in Paris and went to London. After this, Charlie had thought that he wouldn't be seeing her ever again. But little had he known or expected that she would find him once more in his hotel room in London and that he would be forced to abide by her. Charlie was at that time leaving for St. Moritz as Fairbanks had invited him there. He was compelled to bring her along, but when from there he left for Japan, that was really the last time he saw her.

❑

The Hitler Effect

In the late 1920s and early 1930s, Adolf Hitler was not much known by the world at large. Charlie was first introduced to him by his friend, Cornelius Vanderbilt,[182] who was from a wealthy family, but had chosen, much against his family's wishes, to become a newspaper reporter. He was incidentally one of the first to write about Hitler's misdeeds.

"At that time, no one knew much about Hitler's concentration camps. The first intimation of them came from the articles written by my friend Cornelius Vanderbilt, who had, on some pretext, got into one and written of the Nazi tortures there. But his stories of degenerate brutality were so fantastic that few people believed them. Vanderbilt sent me a series of picture postcards showing Hitler making a speech. The face was obscenely comic – a bad imitation of me, with its absurd moustache, unruly, stringy hair and disgusting, thin, little mouth. I could not take Hitler seriously.... The salute with the hand thrown back over the shoulder, the palm upwards, made me want to put a tray of dirty dishes on it. 'This is a nut!' I thought. But when Einstein and Thomas Mann were forced to leave Germany, this face of Hitler was no longer comic but sinister."[183]

When Charlie decided to make a comedy based on Hitler's rule, he was still unaware of a lot of other activities which the Nazis were involved in. That is why, in the movie, the use of the concentration camp does not create much impact as it mostly looked like a normal prison. At that time, Charlie hadn't really known what actually went on inside it. "Had I known of the actual horrors of the German concentration camps, I could not have made *The Great Dictator*; I could not have made fun of the homicidal insanity of the Nazis."[184]

The idea to make a movie on Hitler came to Charlie through his friend, Alexander Korda. In 1937, he proposed to Charlie saying, "I should do a Hitler story based on mistaken identity, Hitler having the same moustache as the tramp: I could play both characters, he said."[185] Charlie had dismissed the thought of it back then.

Charlie's main problem was that he had to make a talkie this time, which is why he was short of ideas. He had been worried that if he now made a talking picture, it wouldn't be as great as his silent ones and that it wouldn't 'surpass the artistry' of his pantomime. Unexpectedly, in a way, it actually did, mainly because this time, the 'story was bigger than the Little Tramp'.[186]

Later, when Charlie was groping for ideas, Alexander's proposal 'suddenly struck' him, and he remembered that Adolf Hitler was a renowned orator and, hence, his dilemma of making a talking picture was resolved. "As Hitler, I could harangue the crowds in jargon and talk all I wanted to. And as the tramp, I could remain more or less silent."[187]

No sooner had Charlie commenced his work on the movie, that he began receiving threats. People told the United Artists that Charlie's new movie would have problems with the censorship board and that he shouldn't really be making such a movie at this hour.

It was an anti-Nazi movie and the diplomats and other officials did not want to risk instigating the war by screening such a movie. The war had not been declared yet, but it was lurking in the corners, waiting for either side to take a wrong step. In such a scenario, *The Great Dictator* could have been that anticipated mistake. Nonetheless, Charlie was not bothered by such threats. "I was determined to go ahead, for Hitler must be laughed at."[188] Certainly, this was before he knew anything about the reality of the concentration camps.

It was during the making of the movie that Charlie lost someone who was extremely precious to him. It was Douglas Fairbanks. He died suddenly of a heart attack, which shocked Charlie and made him feel quite pathetic. He remembered all the good times spent with him and realised that he was going to miss him too much. Before his death, he had come to visit Charlie on the sets and had expressed his enthusiasm about his next movie. Charlie could not believe that now he won't be there to see it. "I have missed Douglas – I have missed the warmth of his enthusiasm and charm; I have missed his friendly voice over the telephone, that used to call me up on a bleak and lonely Sunday morning.... Yes, I have missed his delightful friendship."[189]

While Charlie was yet to complete the movie, Britain and the other Allied Forces declared war on Germany, which gave way to the Second World War. It was September 1939. "How soon we forgot the First World War and its torturous four years of dying. How soon we forgot the appalling human debris: the basket cases – the armless, the legless, the sightless, the jawless, the twisted spastic cripples. Those that were not killed or wounded did not escape, for many were left with deformed minds. Like a minotaur war had gobbled up the youth, leaving cynical old men to survive."[190]

Now Charlie was told to finish his movie fast, as it was the right time to release it. The producers thought that this movie would encourage the people to feel more aggravated towards their enemies.

When the movie was almost done, Charlie received numerous other warnings, where he was told that if he released the movie, they would bomb the theatre or create riots and other such things.

Nonetheless, the movie was released in October 1940. It was first screened for the Press at the Astor. At a meeting, the Press criticised the movie too much, and said that it would lose money. "*The Great Dictator* opened at the Capital to a glamorous audience who were elated and enthused. It stayed fifteen weeks in New York, playing two theatres, and turned out to be the biggest grosser of all my pictures up to that time."[191]

In the movie, Charlie took Paulette as the leading lady, who played the role of Hannah, a Jewish orphan. In the course of its production, they had started having problems in their marriage, but since she was still his friend, their working together didn't create much trouble.

Charlie himself played a double role, that of a Jewish barber from Tomania, and the Dictator of Tomania, Hynkel (a clear imitation of Adolf Hitler).

Charlie's characterisation of Hynkel is one of the most interesting aspects of the movie. Even though he has Hynkel portraying the most dangerous character, he is still shown to be human. "Hitler, for all his wickedness, was not a monster but a man. And the guarantee of Chaplin's seriousness is the way Hynkel is made not a farcical butt but human, and even likable.... Hynkel is at the mercy of his own public image.... His confidence and strength are a sham, his dignity and orderliness continually undermined, his control over events non-existent. At the heart of his character is a fear of his own insignificance."[192] Perhaps Charlie wanted the audience to understand that, above all, peace is the most important thing in the world and that no cause could be so great that one is compelled to take another's life, hence, criticising war.

Another interesting feature of this movie is Hynkel's way of speaking. As has already been said, he is an imitation of Hitler. But what is most amusing is the fact that Charlie is extremely bold in his impersonation. "His histrionic role-playing before the cast crowd is a version of the real Hitler, made comic by additions, exaggerations and refinements. The impersonation is in terms of speech and mannerisms. The gutteral, half-intelligible gobbledegook, with its graduated descent into a coughing fit, that issued from his mouth, suggests, insolently, that this is all Hitler's speeches *are*."[193]

The opening scene of the movie has the Jewish barber, who co-incidentally looks like Hynkel, fighting for his country in the First World War. During the end of the war, he saves Captain Schultz from the enemies but while escaping on a plane, both crash-land, resulting in the barber developing partial amnesia.

When the barber returns to his shop, he doesn't realise until late that the whole scenario has completely changed and that their new ruler, Hynkel was giving a tough time to the Jews. Captain Schultz is still in Hynkel's army and when he sees the barber during one of his rounds of the ghetto, where all the Jews lived, he immediately recognises him, thus, the plot thickens.

In the end, when Schultz turns against the dictator, the latter sends him to the concentration camp, from where he escapes. He comes to the barber for help, but unfortunately, both of them are caught and sent once again to the camp.

The twist in the story occurs when both the men escape and then Hynkel is caught by the officers, who mistake him to be the barber and is, thus, arrested. Meanwhile, the barber is found by some other officers and is thought to be the dictator. He is then asked to give a speech in front of a huge crowd.

What one should know is that the barber is very different from Hynkel. "The contrast in character between Charlie and Hynkel is a moral contrast. The theme of the film is not just the hatefulness of arbitrary and oppressive political power, but its inhuman emptiness. Charlie's world is the human world of domesticity, affectionate relationships and creative activity: Hynkel's is the moral vacuum of hatred, isolation and desperate self-assertion."[194] Thus, the background, from which the barber has come, was unlike that of the dictator and, hence, when he speaks, one can understand why he says what he says.

The speech, with which the movie ends, has the underlying theme of 'Hope'; just as before the speech, Schultz had indicated to the barber, 'This is our only hope', after which the barber repeated in a melancholic tone – 'Hope'.

"I'm sorry but I don't want to be an emperor. That's not my business. I don't want to rule or conquer anyone. I should like to help everyone if possible; Jew, Gentile, black men, white. We all want to help one another. Human beings are like that. We want to live by each others' happiness, not by each other's misery.

We don't want to hate and despise one another. In this world, there is room for everyone. And the good earth is rich and can provide for everyone. The way of life can be free and beautiful, but we have lost the way.

Greed has poisoned men's souls; has barricaded the world with hate; has goose-stepped us into misery and bloodshed. We have developed speed, but we have shut ourselves in. Machinery that gives abundance has left us in want. Our knowledge has made us cynical; our cleverness, hard and unkind. We think too much and feel too little. More than machinery, we need humanity. More than cleverness, we need kindness and gentleness. Without these qualities, life will be violent and all will be lost. The aeroplane and the radio have brought us closer together. The very nature of these inventions cries out for the goodness in man; cries out for universal brotherhood; for the unity of us all.

Even now my voice is reaching millions throughout the world, millions of despairing men, women, and little children, victims of a system that makes men torture and imprison innocent people. To those who can hear me, I say 'Do not despair'. The misery that is now upon us is but the passing of greed, the bitterness of men who fear the way of human progress. The hate of men will pass, and dictators die, and the power they took from the people will return to the people. And so long as men die, liberty will never perish.

Soldiers! Don't give yourselves to brutes, men who despise you and enslave you; who regiment your lives, tell you what to do, what to think and what to feel! Who drill you, diet you, treat you like cattle, use you as cannon fodder! Don't give yourselves to these unnatural men – machine men with machine minds and machine hearts! You are not machines! You are not cattle! You are men! You have a love of humanity in your hearts! You don't hate! Only the unloved hate; the unloved and the unnatural.

Soldiers! Don't fight for slavery! Fight for liberty! In the seventeenth chapter of St. Luke, it's written 'the kingdom of God is within man', not one man nor a group of men, but in all men! In you! You, the people, have the power, the power to create machines, the power to create happiness! You, the people, have the power to make this life free and beautiful, to make this life a wonderful adventure. Then in the name of democracy, let us use that power.

Let us all unite. Let us fight for a new world, a decent world that will give men a chance to work, that will give youth a future and old age a security. By the promise of these things, brutes have risen to power. But they lie! They do not fulfil their promise. They never will! Dictators free themselves but they enslave the people! Now let us fight to fulfil that promise! Let us fight to free the world! To do away with national barriers! To do away with greed, with hate and intolerance! Let us fight for a world of reason, a world where science and progress will lead to all men's happiness.

Soldiers, in the name of democracy, let us all unite!

Hannah, can you hear me? Wherever you are, look up, Hannah. The clouds are lifting. The sun is breaking through. We are coming out of the darkness into the light. We are coming into a new world, a kindlier world, where men will rise above their hate, their greed and brutality. Look up, Hannah. The soul of man has been given wings, and, at last, he is beginning to fly. He is flying into the rainbow – into the light of hope, into the future, the glorious future that belongs to you, to me and to all of us. Look up, Hannah. Look up."[195]

While Charlie is speaking those words, there is a spark in his eyes; he stares out of the screen, as if he is directly sending out a message to his viewers. He talks of peace, liberty, humanity and the upside of unity. He says that the war is over and that it is now time for them to think of a bright future (although, in reality, the war had yet to show its gruesome side).

Through this speech, Charlie is telling his viewers, by referring to Hannah, who represents the people, that there is still hope in this world and that goodwill eventually happens. Charlie's words are so full of passion that one is reminded of his own words, "...acting essentially requires feeling."[196]

But the speech was slammed by the critics. "The New York *Daily News* said I pointed a finger of Communism to the speech and said it was not in character...."[197]

Then Charlie was summoned by the President of the country, Franklin D. Roosevelt, who had only one thing to say to Charlie, that, his movie was becoming a problem for the American Embassy in Argentina.

❑

Going Political

The Great Dictator had created such a sensation all over the world that Charlie did not even realise when he had started drowning in its political sea. The movie undoubtedly was political in every aspect. Since it was an attack on the Nazis, Charlie surely could not have expected to get a smooth response. He knew that the movie would be criticised excessively, but what he did not anticipate was that he too would soon get involved in the administration of the actual war, because of it.

The Unites States of America joined the war wholeheartedly the moment Japan attacked the Pearl Harbour in December 1941. Before this, America was only supporting the Allied Forces; but now, it became somewhat personal. At this point, Russia called for an immediate second front, as they were trying to fight the German army outside Moscow. Roosevelt responded positively, but there were several Nazi supporters in the country, who tried ways and means to create a rift between Russia and America.

Then in May 1942, suddenly Charlie was called upon by the American Committee for the Russian War Relief in San Francisco. They wanted him to give a speech in place of the American Ambassador,

Mr. Davies, who had recently been diagnosed with laryngitis.

Was this too much to ask for? He wasn't a political leader after all. He had nothing to do with politics, except that he had an opinion about it. But naively, Charlie did accept their request, ultimately calling on trouble for himself.

Charlie was to speak in front of a huge crowd and what was worse was that he was their guest of honour.

An extract from the speech, which was published in his autobiography, is as follows, "Comrades! And I mean comrades.... I assume there are many Russians here tonight, and the way your countrymen are fighting and dying at this very moment, it is an honour and a privilege to call you comrades.... I am not a Communist, I am a human being, and I think I know the reactions of human beings. The Communists are no different from anyone else; whether they lose an arm or a leg, they suffer as all of us do, and die as all of us die.... I don't have to be a Communist to know that.... I am here on behalf of Russian war relief.... Money will help, but they need more than money. I am told that the Allies have two million soldiers languishing in the North of Ireland, while Russians alone are facing about two hundred divisions of Nazis.... The Russians are our allies, they are not only fighting for their way of life, but for our way of life and if I know Americans, they like to do their *own* fighting. Stalin wants it, Roosevelt has called for it – so let's call for it – let's open a second front now."[198]

What went wrong was nothing, but for the fact that *he* spoke. Had he said anything different, it wouldn't have mattered, because there were some people who were only waiting to pounce on him, regardless of what he uttered. They were the ones who had called him a Communist from time to time and had criticised his latest movie, just because it reflected the interest of the humanity at large. Charlie ignored them all, not foreseeing his impending doom.

Then Charlie received another request. Since Charlie's first speech was received well by the audience with applause on numerous occasions, he accepted the second offer as well. This time, he had to speak via telephone to a group of people who had gathered in Madison Square. It was a fourteen-minute long speech, an extract of which is thus, "On the battlefields of Russia, democracy will live or die. The fate of the Allied nations is in the hands of the Communists. If Russia is defeated, the Asiatic continent – the largest and richest of this globe – would be under the domination of the Nazis.... With the difficulty of transportation, the problem of our communication lines thousands of miles away, the problem of steel, oil and rubber – and Hitler's strategy of divide and conquer – we would be in a desperate position if Russia should be defeated....

Russians are in desperate need for help. They are pleading for a second front. Among the Allied nations, there is a difference of opinion as to whether a second front is possible now.... But can we afford to wait until we are sure and ready?... If the Russians lose the Caucasus, it will be the greatest disaster of the Allied cause.... Hitler has taken many chances. His biggest one is the Russian campaign.... If Hitler can take chances, can't we? Give us action. Give us more bombs over Berlin...give us a second front now."[199]

Subsequently, Charlie spoke on the issue of the Second Front in a couple of more events, each time praising the Russians and the Communists. "After that, a considerable number of letters came with offers of all kinds.... Now I felt I was caught up in a political avalanche. I began to question my motives: how much was I stimulated by the actor in me and the reaction of a live audience? Would I have entered this quixotic adventure if I had not made an anti-Nazi film? Was it a sublimation of all my irritations and reactions against the talking pictures? I suppose all these elements were involved, but the strongest one was my hate and contempt for the Nazi system."[200]

Charlie's speeches had made the anti-Communists mad, and something in secret was cooking up against him; but no one took any action at that time, as the occasion had demanded unity. Nothing happened for at least a few more years, up till the war ended in 1945.

"Chaplin's final speech in favour of the Soviet-American alliance against fascism was at a dinner in his honour on 3 December 1942, at Pennsylvania Hotel in New York City. It was given by the 'Arts to Russia Week' committee of Russian War Relief.... This gathering made it clear that the Soviets had embraced Chaplin as a 'people's artist', whether he sought the title or not, and that Chaplin himself was willing to praise publically the Soviet effort against the Nazis. Throughout his six speeches in 1942, Chaplin gradually, perhaps imperceptibly to him, moved from a focus on the necessity to oppose the Nazi threat to a tendency to praise the Soviet allies and urge closer ties with them. In the context of the war effort in 1942, such praise was not uncommon.... But when the political climate changed, Chaplin would be called upon to answer for his actions."[201]

❑

An Episode with Joan Barry

In the middle of all this, a controversy in the life of Charlie Chaplin took place. It came in the form of Joan Barry. She was a friend of his friend and had insisted on meeting with Charlie. "The lady in question was pleasant and cheerful enough and the four of us spent an innocuous evening together and I never thought of seeing her again."[202]

But he did see her again, and on numerous other occasions thereafter. Charlie claimed that she used to call him several times unexpectedly and ask him to meet her, to which he had to oblige, as he saw no harm in it. But when sometimes, even without calling, she showed up at his house in the middle of the night, he began to worry.

Then one day, Joan showed interest in acting. Charlie took a screen test of her, to see if she was any good. She wanted to act in a film adaptation of the play, *Shadow and Substance*. When he saw that she had potential, Charlie bought the film rights and admitted Joan into an acting school.

What followed was a series of unfortunate events which involved Joan getting drunk and driving in the late hours of the night on the streets. She also began smashing the windows of his house. Charlie did not understand why she was doing this, but the fact that this could pose a serious threat to the image of the Chaplin Studios, bothered him. "Overnight, my existence became a nightmare."[203] Then she told Charlie that she did not want to become an actress anymore and demanded some money to leave the matter as it is. Charlie paid her the amount and 'was glad to be rid of her'.

Little did he know that she would soon be coming back in his life and that too with a renewed sense of purpose. "At 1:00 a.m. on December 23 (1942), after her few knocks and rings had gone unanswered, Barry forced herself into Chaplin's home by breaking two windows. Gun in hand, she went to Chaplin's second floor bedroom, where she held him at gunpoint and threatened suicide. This incident – corroborated by Chaplin, Barry's courtroom testimony, and Chaplin's sons – was not settled until the morning, when Chaplin managed to get the gun from Barry and persuaded her to leave."[204]

This had happened a few months after Charlie had supposedly gotten rid of her. It was nothing new in what she had done, but since she was doing it all over again, Charlie felt threatened. He called the police and tried to have her arrested immediately, but the police left her by only giving a mild warning. Then a few weeks later, when she again came back to Charlie's house, she was arrested but soon released after she promised to leave him alone.

Had this been the end of Barry's chapter, it wouldn't have been that big a drama. But it wasn't. Just when Charlie thought that it was finally over, and that he could go on with his life now, Barry took him through another adventure, and this time, it also involved the judiciary.

"The affair seemed to have settled until Barry, pregnant, returned to Los Angeles in May. She tried to see Chaplin in order to claim that she was pregnant with his child. On 7 May 1943, following Chaplin's complaint, she was arrested by the Beverly Hills police for violating the terms of her probation and jailed."[205]

What happened after that was anticipated but not to such an extent. "A few hours later, the newspapers were black with headlines. I was pilloried, excoriated and vilified: Chaplin, the father of her unborn child, had had her arrested, had left her destitute. A week later, a paternity suit was brought against me."[206]

It was much later that Charlie came to know about her going to the Press, who, in turn, had advised her to get arrested, just so that she could garner some sympathy from the public.

Charlie called up Lloyd Wright to fight his paternity case. The lawyer suggested that a simple blood-test can determine whether Charlie could be the father of that child or not. "Later he (Wright) came with the news that he had reached an agreement with her lawyer. The terms were that if we gave Joan Barry $25,000, she and her child would submit to a blood-test, and if the test proved that I could not be the father, she would drop the paternity suit. I leaped at the offer."[207]

Then Charlie got wind that something else was brewing apart from Barry's paternity case, when he heard that the Federal Government had got involved and was questioning Barry about her intentions.

The next thing Charlie knew was that he was being charged with four different violations by the Federal Government. Two of them were of the Mann Act and the other two were of some Act which his lawyer said was considered to be obsolete. Charlie in his autobiography claimed that these cases were just the government's way of getting back at him for his second front speeches. "Every once in a while the Federal Government used this bit of legal blackmail to discredit a political opponent.... Should a man accompany his divorced wife over the border to another state, and should he have intercourse with her, he has committed an offence against the Mann Act and is liable to five years in prison. It was this bogus piece of legal opportunism upon which the United States brought an indictment against me."[208]

As a desperate measure, Wright involved Giesler, who was a renowned criminal lawyer. Both of them were pretty confident that they would win all the cases.

Charlie's trial soon began and it was a tough routine. His major concern now had become to get rid of the cases as soon as possible and resume work. He was unable to concentrate either on *Shadow and Substance* or *Monsieur Verdoux*. In the meantime, Barry's child grew up and was ready to give the blood test. The results showed that Charlie was not the father. This was the only piece of good news that had come to them in months.

Then Charlie got to know that the second two charges of violation on him were dropped due to some unknown technicalities. Now only the Mann Act was left, which was taking a lot of Charlie's time.

"Besides the tension and worry of the trial, there was the boring routine of getting up at seven in the morning, then having to leave immediately after breakfast because it was an hour's drive through Los Angeles traffic, and to be strictly on time, ten minutes before the court opened."[209]

Finally, when the trial came to an end, Charlie was relieved. It was the day of his judgement and somehow it seemed as a very long day. When the verdict came out, it was after several hours but they were all in favour of Charlie. After all the drama, how did the government let him go free, Charlie did not understand, but since he knew that he was innocent, he did not show much emotion.

One could not believe that Charlie had gone through so much in such a short time. All that he had now wanted was to be left alone. However, before Charlie could breathe some fresh air, one last torture unexpectedly crept in like a snake but that was it.

"And now the paternity case which I thought had been disposed of by the blood-test loomed up again. By adroit finagling, another lawyer, influential in local politics, was able to reopen the case; by his tricky device of transferring the guardianship of the child from the mother to the court.... So, now the court as guardian was able to sue me for the support of the child."[210]

Unfortunately, this verdict went against him and Charlie lost the case.

❑

Monsieur and His Bride

Charlie's fourth wife was Oona O'Neill, the daughter of the well-known playwright, Eugene O'Neill. How and under what circumstances Charlie first met her is something he would never have wanted to remember, but since the day he saw her, it was magic for him.

Charlie had been working on *Shadow and Substance* without having a leading lady, since Barry had just left him, saying that she did not want to become an actress. Then Orson Welles came to him with a proposal which gave Charlie another movie idea. Welles wanted to cast him in his documentary about the notorious French murderer, Bluebeard Landru.

Although Charlie refused to participate because he was also asked to write its script, he asked Welles, whether he could use the character of Landru to make his own movie, to which the latter agreed. This way, *Shadow and Substance* was shelved and Charlie began his work on *Monsieur Verdoux*.

Then one day, Miss Wallace, a Hollywood agent called up Charlie and suggested Oona O'Neill for the role of the leading lady in *Shadow and Substance*. Charlie was not much keen on meeting her, as she had no experience in acting. Nevertheless, Miss Wallace invited him for dinner and told him that she would also be there.

"I arrived early and, on entering the sitting-room, discovered a young lady seated alone by the fire. While waiting for Miss Wallace, I introduced myself, saying I presumed she was Miss O'Neill. She smiled. Contrary to my preconceived impression, I became aware of a luminous beauty, with a sequestered charm and a gentleness that was most appealing."[211]

But Oona was seventeen at that time, which made it difficult for Charlie to decide on whether to take her, since he wanted an older woman, because the role was a bit complex. Although when he got to know that she was getting a film offer from the Fox Film Company, he immediately signed her.

Gradually, as and when Charlie got to know Oona, he realised that she was much more matured than her age showed. "I was constantly surprised by her sense of humour and tolerance; she could always see the other person's point of view. This and multitudinous other reasons were why I fell in love with her."[212]

Charlie was now working on *Shadow and Substance* as soon as Oona was selected to play its leading lady. He kept *Monsieur Verdoux* aside for now, as he thought it required much more time and energy and that he would complete it after *Shadow and Substance.*

It was during this time that Barry's legal episode happened. Charlie was much in love with Oona and since she was now over eighteen, they had even talked about getting married.

So, while Barry was filing a paternity suit on Charlie, he ran away with Oona to Carpinteria[213] in order to get married.[214] "But before we could obtain the license, we had to register at the Santa Barbara town hall.... The register clerk, if one of the couples happens to be celebrated, usually notifies the newspapers by pressing a secret button under the desk.... When I appeared he took it big.... Just as we left the building and were entering our car, the Press drove into the courtyard. From then on it was a race for life...we evaded them and arrived in Carpinteria, where Oona and I were quietly married."[215]

Charlie and Oona then stayed in Santa Barbara in a rented house for about two months. They wanted peace as the Barry episode had much frustrated him.

During this time, Charlie felt lost, as everything was working against him. Often he used to get depressed, thinking that his work on the two films was not progressing and the whole country had started to hate him as they thought him to be a criminal, thanks to the Press. "At such times, Oona would lift me out of this mood by reading *Trilby* to me.... In spite of an occasional depression, those two months in Santa Barbara were poignantly romantic, motivated by bliss, anxiety and despair."[216]

Oona was four months pregnant when Charlie's Mann Act verdict came out. And when all the cases were finally over, Charlie took Oona to Nyack, where they stayed for a while in a rented house. The house, Charlie described, was built in 1780 and was small and beautiful. Charlie, at that time, owned a black kitten and when they arrived in the rented house, he saw that the housekeeper had an old black retriever.[217] Both the animals had great fun together, playing the usual cat and dog game.

Charlie and Oona enjoyed their stay in Nyack, mainly because there was no one to disturb them there. He had also almost completed his work on *Monsieur Verdoux* and was now eager to get back and finish it.

Charlie had completely dropped the idea of making *Shadow and Substance* soon after their marriage, when Oona told him that she was no more interested in acting. "This news pleased me, for, at last, I had a wife and not a career girl. It was then that I abandoned *Shadow and Substance* and went back to work on *Monsieur Verdoux* – until I was so rudely interrupted by the Government."[218]

Once back home, Charlie soon finished his script. It had taken him years to get to it and he wasn't much pleased about it. But when the shooting was done, he was satisfied, as that had not taken much time.

After finishing a movie, it was compulsory that the filmmaker sends his script to the censor board for their reviewing. And that is exactly what Charlie did with *Monsieur Verdoux*. But what he didn't know at the time was that they would completely strip his film of its dignity.

Charlie had sent his script to the Breen Office, which was a branch of the Legion of Decency, the official board for censorship for the Motion Picture Association. They wrote him back saying that they wish to ban the film from releasing. "The Breen Office... initially disapproved the script in its entirety, claiming that it 'impugns the present-day social structure' – even though the story was set in France between the two World Wars. In the end, they were satisfied with only a few cuts, though the prudery of those times demanded the removal of all scenes that suggested that a husband and wife might share the same bed or that a girl was a prostitute."[219]

Charlie's own thoughts on censorship were as follows, "From a moral point of view, I believe that physical violence and false philosophy are as harmful as a lurid sex scene. Bernard Shaw said that punching a villain on the jaw is too easy a way of solving life's problems."[220]

Monsieur Verdoux was a film based on the real life of an infamous French murderer, Monsieur Landru. Charlie had written nothing extraordinary. The fact that the story is of a man, who kills more than ten women and rips them off their money, in itself shows how much censorship that could have required. Charlie was ahead of his time and the audience wasn't ready for such a film. As he himself had commented, that this movie was "the cleverest and most brilliant film I have yet made."[221]

"*Monsieur Verdoux* is subtitled 'a comedy of murder'. Both halves of this equation deserve equal weight. The comedy is as important as the murder: indeed, the murders themselves are comic – or, at least, the preparations for them, which are all we are usually allowed to see."[222]

The movie is about a respectable bank clerk named Henri Verdoux, who loses his job when the Depression strikes. This results him into finding a job for himself. What does he end up doing? Marrying middle-aged single ladies and robbing them off after killing them. This, he called to himself, as his 'profession'. The first impression of this man is that he is perhaps very ruthless. It comes as a surprise when he is shown with an actual wife and a son, whom he loves very much and lies to them about his unemployment.

The story ends with him being caught by the police, which looked more like Verdoux surrendering himself while making it appear as he's being trapped by the crowd. Verdoux in the ending scene justifies his murders in his court trial by comparing them to the mass killings during the Second World War. "Chaplin uses the story to make a satirical comparison between private and public murder. Verdoux declares at his trial, 'As for being a mass murderer, does not the world encourage it? Is it not building weapons of destruction for the sole purpose of mass killing?' and tells a reporter who comes to interview him in the death cell, 'One murder makes a villain.... Millions a hero. Numbers sanctify, my good friend.' Sentiments like these were deeply suspect in 1940's America, which had already begun to slide into the paranoia and witch-hunting of the Cold War years."[223]

United Artists at this point in time was incurring heavy losses. Charlie was confident that his new movie would help them recover everything. Meanwhile, almost everyone had left the company and since Douglas had died, Mary Pickford was the only one left to share the ownership with Charlie. This made the matters worse as now they were each having fifty percent partnership in a drowning company.

When *Monsieur Verdoux* was released in April 1947, there was a swarm of people at its premiere and Charlie was confident of its success, but as soon as he went in, he found that the air inside was a little tense. "The moment the film started, instead of the eager anticipation and the happy stir of the past that had greeted my films, there was a nervous applause scattered with a few hisses.... As the picture progressed, I began to get worried. The laughter was there but divided.... My heart began to sink."[224]

The movie received mixed reactions from the audience and unexpectedly did good business in the first six weeks, but then, all of a sudden, something happened. When he asked his officials of United Artists, they told him that all his movies always do well in its first few weeks because of his loyal fans; but after that, the general public comes in, who are the ones who actually decide the fate of a movie.

Such was the plight of United Artists that they were now ready to even sell the company which they had nurtured for so many years. Thus, over the years, it went through the hands of several people, and currently is owned wholly by the MGM Company.

❑

The Outsider

"How does it feel to be an artist who has enriched the world with so much happiness and understanding of the little people, and to be derided and held up to hate and scorn by the so-called representatives of the American Press?"[225]

These words, spoken by the American poet and novelist, Jim Agee, in a Press Conference for *Monsieur Verdoux*, actually say a lot about an artist's position in a society which is not ready to accept his thoughts.

Unfortunately, when Charlie was asked this question, he was not in a state of mind to give a proper answer, as he had been surrounded by an angry Press, who were acting exactly as Mr. Agee had suggested. Hence, the question in itself became rhetorical.

Charlie, during this point in time, had become a victim of bad press. He did not expect any of them to like him anymore. Was this happening to him just because he made *The Great Dictator*? Or was it because he had dared to say anything in favour of Communism in front of a huge crowd? Some say, it was also because of the publicity of the paternity suit trial of Joan Barry's child which created this confusion among the people.

David Robinson clearly stated, "Chaplin was not, of course, America's enemy, but, in the character of Monsieur Verdoux he was undoubtedly a critic, in a society in which criticism was deeply unwelcome."[226]

The result, as expected, was that Charlie Chaplin, the man who had made America laugh, was now being called an outsider by the same people. Some even had the audacity to ask him why he hadn't yet become a citizen of the country, to which he simply replied – "I consider myself a citizen of the world."[227]

Then out of nowhere came up the plagiarism suit on Charlie for his movie *The Great Dictator*; "...at the height of the intense hate and antagonism of both the Press and the public, and while four senators were denouncing me on the floor of the Senate, the case was tried with a jury, in spite of my wanting to postpone it."[228]

Incidentally, during that time, the Senators had also been charging him of un-American activities, ever since he had spoken in support of the Russians in his second front speeches. Charlie had replied to their summons as thus, "I am not a Communist, neither have I ever joined a political party or organisation in my life. I am what you call 'a peace-monger'."[229]

The plagiarism suit was ultimately settled out of court since Charlie was tired of attending trials and wanted to get over with it as soon as possible.

"Not surprisingly, then, in choosing his next subject, he deliberately sought escape from disagreeable contemporary reality. He found it in bitter-sweet nostalgia for the world of his youth – the world of the London music halls at the opening of the 20th century, where he had first discovered his genius as an entertainer."[230]

Limelight (October 1952) was Charlie's next movie, which opens with a scene of 1914 London, when the music halls had played the biggest part in the entertainment of the society. It was before this time that Calvero, a clown, had achieved fame and was now forgotten.

This was regrettably the last movie that Charlie made while he was still in America.

Charlie had got the ideà to make this film after he got inspired by the life of Frank Tinney, a well-known comedian of his time, who had suffered a downfall later in his life. "I saw him again on the stage a few years later and was shocked for the comic Muse had left him. He was so self-conscious that I could not believe it was the same man. It was this change in him that gave me the idea years later for my film *Limelight*. In *Limelight* the case was age; Calvero grew old and introspective and acquired a feeling of dignity, and this divorced him from all intimacy with the audience."[231]

The music in *Limelight* was composed by Charlie himself. The toughest part was that this time he was to write the music for a twelve-minute ballet piece before seeing the dance itself. Ballet was one of the main themes of the movie as *Limelight* was a story of love between a clown and a ballerina. "Eventually Melissa Hayden,[232] the ballerina, and André Eglevsky flew out to Hollywood to hear it.... It was one of the thrilling moments of my film career to see them dance to it. Their interpretation was most flattering and gave the music a classic significance."[233]

The movie essentially holds a melancholic tone throughout, with very little comedy thrown in between. Even the leading lady's entry into the movie is sad, as the first scene shows her being found by Calvero, who has broken into her room after smelling a gas leakage only to find her lying in bed with an empty bottle of poison in her hand.

The parts which are actually funny, happen mostly in Calvero's dreams, which suddenly turn out to become nightmares, as he sees an empty hall with no applause after his performance is over.

Limelight, as the name suggests, is all about the limelight and what it does to a man when his time is over.

In the end, it only seems fitting that Calvero dies of a heart attack, after giving his last performance, which receives great appreciation. This final act was such that the public could not get enough of him, and that is how he wanted to be remembered.

"This is the famous double act with Buster Keaton, in which, as would-be *salon* musicians, their efforts to produce music are repeatedly frustrated by the malevolence of their instruments, or of their own bodies. This scene has a more vivid life than Calvero's earlier performances, and has always been recognized as crucial to the film. It is difficult now to place it *within* the film, so direct is its real-life appeal."[234]

After Charlie had finished *Limelight*, he decided to go to Europe once again. He understood that America had no enthusiasm left for his movies, so he resolved to have the premiere of his movie in London. By this time, he and Oona together had four children – Geraldine, Michael, Josephine and Victoria. It was for them too that they were going, since Oona wanted them to have their schooling away from the surroundings of Hollywood.

Hence, Charlie applied for a permit for re-entry. Had he known the scenario at full-length, he wouldn't have even bothered to do so and would have immediately packed his bags and left America forever. But he didn't and, therefore, he applied.

"I had made an application for a re-entry permit three months previously but had received no reply.... My taxes had been filed and they had all been cleared.

But when the Internal Revenue Service heard that I was leaving for Europe, they discovered I owed them more money.... My instinct told me to put up nothing and to insist on the case coming to court immediately. This bought a quick settlement for a very nominal sum."[235]

After clearing the matter of taxes, Charlie again applied for his re-entry, but when he did not receive any answer, he directly sent a letter to Washington regarding this matter.

This time the Immigration Department instantly called him to ask if they could come to his house for questioning. They were being so extremely polite, that Charlie suspected them a little, but he dismissed that thought immediately, after reflecting on what could possibly go wrong anyway.

They interrogated Charlie for about three hours, asking him his real name and place of birth, which Charlie contemplated was a bit strange. Then they asked him the same question which the Press had been asking regarding his involvement in the Communist Party.

Charlie answered each of their questions with appropriate answers after which they left saying nothing. However, a week later, they called up again and asked him to come to their office. To his surprise, this time, there was no more delay in anything and after asking him about the length of his stay in Europe, they gave him the permit.

Journey across the Ocean

It was now time for Charlie to leave. But even during his last days in America, he was not left alone in peace. "Just as I was preparing to enjoy myself, my lawyer, Charles Schwartz, called up to say that an ex-employee of United Artists was suing the company.... So, for the last four days, I was confined to my room."[236]

Charlie, thus, had to board his ship quite early in the morning to avoid the process-servers. "My lawyer's instructions were to steal aboard, lock myself in my suite and not to appear on deck until the pilot disembarked. Being groomed for the last ten years to expect the worst, I obeyed."[237]

When the ship sailed, Charlie came out of his room and breathed some fresh air. For some reason, he felt freer now, because for the first time in his life, after becoming a star, was he sailing to Europe with a family that he loved, with the sole purpose of having fun. "No longer was I a myth of the film world, or a target of acrimony, but a married man with a wife and family on a holiday."[238]

Charlie and Oona decided to spend the rest of their days on the ship, without worrying about anything. The past was over, and they wanted to forget everything about it. No sooner had they thought this that a fresh problem arrived. A few days into the journey, Harry Crocker, who handled Charlie's public affairs, received a telegram which stated that Charlie was banned from re-entering the United States of America on grounds of his political and moral depravity.

It was much later that they came to know that J. Edgar Hoover,[239] who had been keeping secret files on Charlie's activities ever since the early 1930s, had arranged for the cancellation of his permit after hearing about his Europe tour.

While still on board, when Charlie was told that the United Press wanted to know his view on this matter, his tolerance level was gone, but with much effort, he retained his composure. "I would like to have told them that the sooner I was rid of that hate-beleaguered atmosphere, the better, that I was fed up with America's insults and moral pomposity, and that the whole subject was damned boring. But everything I possessed was in the States and I was terrified they might find a way of confiscating it.... So, instead I came out with a pompous statement to the effect that I would return and answer their charges, and that my re-entry permit was not a 'scrap of paper', but a document given to me in good faith by the United States Government."[240]

The moment Charlie arrived in London, everyone went after him to know what he thought about the American Government and his recent banishment from the country. He had a lot to say to them, but he was saving it for later, waiting first to have all that he owned, safely out of that country.

A lot had changed in London in the last twenty years; Charlie could now see a lot of America's influence on its streets such as the 'lunch counters, hot-dog stands and milk bars...hatless youths and blue-jeaned girls'. He took Oona through Pownall Terrace and Kennington Road, and showed her all that he had gone through as a child.

Oona then hurriedly flew to California to clear their Bank accounts and bring back everything that she could from their house. "She was away for ten days. When she returned, she told me in detail what had happened. At the bank, the clerk studied her signature, looked at her, then left and had quite a conference with the bank manager. Oona had a moment of uneasiness until they opened our deposit box.... Then, later, she saw Henry, our Swiss butler, who told her that when she went away, the F.B.I. men had called twice and interrogated him, wanting to know what kind of a man I was."[241]

Once Oona was back in London, Charlie was free to proclaim his hatred towards the American society and their government. Now whenever anyone asked him why he was so opposed to them, he would give a three-fold reply. First, he would say that he was against the American Legion because they always went beyond what the law has allowed them as they "...under the guise of patriotism use their power to encroach upon others, then they commit an offence against the fundamental structure of the American Government. Such super patriots could be the cells to turn America into a fascist state."[242]

Next, he would say that he did not like the Committee of Un-American Activities, as it was "a dishonest phrase to begin with, elastic enough to wrap around the throat and strangle the voice of any American citizen, whose honest opinion is a minority one."[243]

The third point included why he never tried to become a citizen of America. His reason was valid enough; "...scores of Americans earning their living in England have never attempted to become British subjects...and the British have never bothered about it."[244]

❑

Life Beyond America

Charlie's premiere of *Limelight* in London was a success. No matter how strongly the Americans tried to bury his film in their country, Charlie still had the rest of the world as his audience.

The verification of this fact came from the letter that Charlie received from the President of Société des Auteurs et Compositeurs Dramatiques, Roger Ferdinand. From London, Charlie had gone to Paris, where he was honoured with several awards. An extract of the letter, which Mr. Ferdinand wrote to Charlie, is as follows, "Should certain people be surprised at the publicity given to your presence here, they would be ill-acquainted with the reasons for which we love and admire you; they would also be very bad judges of human values, and would not have taken the trouble to count the blessings that you have heaped upon us during the last forty years, nor have appreciated your teaching, or the quality of the joys and emotions that you have lavished upon us, at their true worth; to say the least they would be thoroughly grateful. You are among the greatest personalities of the world and your claim to fame is equal to that of those who can be placed among the most illustrious.... Today, our Society of Authors and Dramatists has the honour and joy of welcoming you.... We are most anxious to receive you into our midst and to tell you how much we admire and love you, and also to say that you are really one of us."[245]

In Paris, Charlie also met with Jean-Paul Sartre and Picasso. Charlie, in his autobiography, described them as thus, "Picasso has a quizzical, humorous look, and could pass for an acrobat or a clown more readily than a painter. Sartre had a round face and, although his features do not bear analysis, they have a subtle beauty and sensitiveness."[246] Then Charlie gave an account of Picasso's studio, which he was fortunate enough to have entered. "We came upon the most deplorable, barnlike garret.... Hanging from a nail in one rafter was a stark electric bulb, which enabled us to see a rickety old iron bed and a broken-down stove. Resting against the wall was a pile of old dusty canvases. He picked up one – a Cézanne, and a most beautiful one. He picked up another and another. We must have looked at fifty masterpieces... In that, Gorki's 'lower depth' was a gold mine."[247]

Next Charlie went to Rome. The premiere in France had gone really well and he was hoping for the same in Italy. But, unfortunately, during the premiere, even after being warned by the organisers, he purposely went through the area which was more crowded. So when he got out of his car, a group of young boys threw tomatoes at him.

"Then the humour of the situation struck me and I could not stop laughing.... Later, we learned that the offenders were young neo-fascists."[248] Charlie, for a moment, had forgotten that Italy was a part of the 'Triple Alliance' in the two World Wars, and, hence, an enemy of Britain and the other Allied Forces.

Off to Switzerland

Charlie was now resolved into finding new place for his family. He did not want to settle in London as he found that this city was not appropriate for his children. Then someone told him to go to Switzerland which immediately caught Charlie's fancy.

Thus, after saying their final goodbye to the thought of returning to America, the family packed their bags and headed towards Switzerland, where they stayed in a hotel for some time.

It was 1953 and Oona was about to have her fifth child, and since she did not want to live in a hotel after the baby came, Charlie had to hurry. After a few months of hunting, he found a beautiful house, by the name of Manior de Ban, in Corsier, which is a small village near Vevey. "To our amazement, we discovered that it had thirty-seven acres, with an orchard, which, among other things, produces large black cherries, delicious green plums, apples and pears; and a vegetable garden that grows strawberries and wonderful asparagus and corn, to which, in season, no matter where we are, we make a special pilgrimage. In front of the terrace is a five-acre lawn with magnificent tall trees, which frame the mountains and the lake in the distance."[249]

This soon became Charlie's new home where he stayed for the rest of his life along with his wife Oona and their eight children (four of whose names have already been mentioned and the others are – Eugene, Jane, Annette and Christopher).

Meanwhile, Charlie had become so fond of this place now that Oona too decided to give up her citizenship of America. So, with this purpose, they went to London and entered the American Embassy. By now, Charlie had no expectations of friendly behaviour from the American people. But when one of their officials asked him to come in and told him about how he had first seen him in 1911 at the Empress Theatre, Charlie's antagonism subsided a bit and they started talking about the old times.

Next day, while Oona and Charlie were having dinner, they suddenly saw Winston Churchill coming towards their table. He had seen his *Limelight* and had much liked it. Churchill then reminded Charlie about a letter which he had written to him a few years ago, to congratulate him on his last film. He had seemed rather offended that Charlie never replied back. "I was charmed with the great man's modesty in remembering that unanswered letter of two years ago. But I have never seen eye to eye with his politics."[250]

After coming back, Charlie decided to settle everything that was still left in America for him. He, therefore, dissolved all his American companies and liquidated the shares that he had in any of them. Apart from that, he also stopped paying the salary to all those who were still employed under him, including his maid and butler. "All those who worked for me in California were still on salary, but I could not afford to continue paying them now that I was domiciled in Switzerland. So, I arranged for their severance pay, giving each a bonus."[251] This, of course, took some time, but ultimately, in about a year, he straightened up all his accounts, and could now look forward to a life beyond America.

Edna Purviance was the only one whom Charlie continued to pay up till the day she died. Maybe it was because he always had a soft corner for her, but this, only he could know. She died in January 1958.

He had now started to loathe his previous country of occupation, basically because it had changed a lot since he had first stepped on its soil. He did not miss it anymore. "The gigantic scale of industrial institutions, of Press, television and commercial advertising has completely divorced me from the American way of life."[252]

Throughout his life, Charlie had met numerous legendary personalities who could have also said the same thing about him. Though after settling in Switzerland, he hardly got to meet any of them. Sometimes, the family visited other cities, which gradually became a kind of a tradition for them. "During Easter holidays, we take the children to the south of Ireland.... Often on the spur of the moment, we decide to go to London and Paris, sometimes to Venice or Rome."[253] It was only when they were on such holidays, that they encountered some of their old friends and other eminent people, who would then invite them for parties or dinners.

In Switzerland though, Charlie once had the opportunity to meet India's first Prime Minister, Jawaharlal Nehru and his daughter, Indira Gandhi. They had come to Switzerland for some purpose of their own, when Charlie arranged a meeting with them. Upon meeting Nehru, Charlie asked him about what ideological direction was India heading towards, to which the man replied, "In whatever direction, it is for the betterment of the Indian people."[254]

Charlie also met Chou En-lai, the first Premier of the People's Republic of China, in Geneva. This meeting happened to take place when the Chinese Embassy called up Charlie and asked him if they could have a screening of *City Lights* in Geneva for Chou En-lai. Charlie obviously agreed and was, thus, invited to have dinner with him. "At dinner, we drank Chinese champagne, and like the Russians, made many toasts. I toasted the future of China and said that although I was not a Communist, I wholeheartedly joined in their hope and desire for a better life for the Chinese people, and for all people."[255]

❑

His Final Years

The Last Two Films

In 1957, *A King in New York*, apparently the last movie where Charlie played a leading role, was released. He was almost seventy now but still had the capacity to make people laugh.

He started conceptualising the movie in the early 1950s, right after all the money matters had been settled, and he came to live in Switzerland. Charlie had great difficulty in making this film, as it was the first time that he had to make a movie outside the comforts of his own studio (except when during his early days, he was working for other companies). "To take up film making again, as an exile, was a challenging undertaking. For almost forty years, he had enjoyed the luxury of his own studio and a staff of regular employees, who understood his way of work. Now though he had to work with strangers, in costly and unfriendly rented studios. In the old days, he could take all the time he wanted, trying things over and over again until he got them to his satisfaction. Now every minute cost money. Working under such constraints, Chaplin completed shooting *A King in New York* in what was for him a record time of only twelve weeks."[256] Although he did finish the movie quite fast, the main problem was that this hastiness in the shooting and the acting was quite evident when one watched the movie.

A lot has been said about this movie being a medium through which Charlie condemns the American society. Probably, it is true, as in the movie one does see him making fun of American commercials and social pretentions.

Charlie plays the role of King Igor Shahdov, who is in America on an exile, as his theories on Atomic power led him to be banned from his own country. There is a stark resemblance between this story and Charlie's own; and the perpetual theme of Communism which looms around in the background, makes it even more obvious to the audience that it was more about him than about anything else. This probably could be seen as the answer that Charlie gave to the American Government for his own banishment.

Apart from Charlie, Michael Chaplin, his eldest son with Oona, also played a key role in the movie, whose parents are shown to be Communists. Charlie, through his mouth, speaks everything that he himself wanted to say. "Do I have to be a Communist to read Karl Marx?" These few words spoken by the character of Michael, questioned the very foundations of the pretentious society that America had come to exist in, after the two World Wars. It was the period of Cold War, when America had tried to ban everything that reflected the thought of Communism.

The film, as predicted, received heavy criticism from the American Press. "*Time*, for example, opened its review by telling its readers that Chaplin was a 'bitter man' and a 'self exile' settled in Switzerland: 'Convinced that he had been persecuted by McCarthyism, Red-liner Chaplin decided to deprive the

U.S. of one of the few authentic geniuses produced by the movies.' *Time* then prefaced a plot summary with a sharp critique of its politics: 'Intended as satire, *King's* few funny spots are outweighed by shrill invective and heavy-footed propaganda.' .... Similarly, the *New Republic* minimized (or side-stepped) the validity of the political critique by finding fault with the presentation of the material: 'Chaplin leads us clumsily towards the point of the film – McCarthyism[257] – by introducing a repugnant little schoolboy, played by his son.'"[258] The movie was not screened in America until 1967.

In Europe, the movie was released in 1957, but it wasn't as successful, as all the other Chaplin films had been in the past; but here, the reason had been quite different; the fault lied in the technique of the film and not in its political drama, as the reviewers called it, 'not funny enough'.

Charlie's last film, *A Countess from Hong Kong* was released in 1967, starring Marlon Brando and Sophia Loren. It was also his only film which was made in colour. Charlie merely directed the movie and did not lead in it, although he played a cameo, as the ship's steward. His three eldest daughters, Geraldine, Josephine and Victoria also appeared in the movie for a very short duration. Moreover, the film featured Sydney Earl Chaplin, who was Charlie's second son from his second wife, Lita Grey.

After Retirement

Now that Charlie had retired from the film world, he spent his life peacefully in his home in Switzerland with his family of ten (Oona and their eight children), meeting neighbours, and sometimes visiting other countries and catching up with his old friends.

Before Charlie's last film was released, the news of his brother's death came to him. Sydney died on April 16, 1965, in his last place of residence, Nice, France. He was eighty years old and had been suffering from an illness. It was quite a loss for his younger brother as Sydney had been his first best friend, with whom he had spent his entire childhood in extreme poverty, and at a time, when they had nothing to look forward to in life. Sydney was buried in Clarens-Montreux Cemetery, which is near Vevey.

In the same year, Geraldine, Charlie's eldest daughter, became a star after playing a leading role in the movie *Doctor Zhivago*. She later also played the role of Charlie's mother Hannah, in *Chaplin*, which was a film based on Charlie's life. *Chaplin* was released in 1992, and starred Robert Downey Jr. in the role of Charlie Chaplin.

Charlie, during the 1930s, apart from creating magic as a director, was also involved in writing a book about his own life. The book is titled *My Autobiography*, and was released in September 1964. It is a detailed description of his life as he remembers, and it contains an account of almost all the events that he has experienced since his childhood till about the mid-1950s, where he ends the book, giving the readers a picture of his calm and peaceful life in Switzerland, away from the hassles of America.

It was during this time that Charlie's name in America was beginning to get restored. People, after about more than a decade, were starting to realise their mistake, as soon as the clouds of Red-Scare were moving away. "On the broadest plane, the ideology of liberal consensus that had dominated American intellectual and political life since the late 1940s, began to break down. Many came to question its basic assumptions and, increasingly, to accept those who, like Chaplin, challenged them."[259]

The other factors that helped Charlie in gaining back the admiration of the people of America were some of his own doings. The publication of his autobiography was one of them.

After *A King in New York* was released, he obtained the help of his legal representatives, who then worked their way through the federal courts and claimed the rights of all his movies, which were made under First National and United Artists. Next, Charlie organised a screening of all his old feature films in New York; this eventually facilitated in the revival his lost glory and also brought with it a new generation of fan following, who instantly fell in love with him. "By running three of Chaplin's best First National films and all of the comic features through *The Great Dictator* except *The Circus*, the schedule brought to the fore the Charlie persona, who originally did so much to establish Chaplin as a star in Hollywood. Then, by playing *Verdoux* and the autobiographical *Limelight*, the series enabled viewers who saw all the films to examine them as examples of how Chaplin the director and actor evolved after he felt compelled to abandon the Charlie persona."[260]

The Special Oscar

In the year 1972, twenty years after his exile, when Charlie was almost eighty-three, he received his first Oscar for the "incalculable effect in making motion pictures the art form of the century". This happened when Moses Rothman, an American studio executive, suggested that the best possible way in which Charlie could gain maximum publicity for his films, that were being rereleased since the past few years, was by returning to America. Charlie agreed and, thus, the inevitable happened.

"The return became a major media event. On January 13 (1972), Motion Picture Academy president, Daniel Taradash announced that Chaplin would attend the Oscar ceremonies in April to receive a special Oscar."[261]

Charlie arrived in New York with his family on April 3, where he received a beautiful reception. The next day, the Film Society of the Lincoln Centre funded the screenings of a few of his films in Philharmonic Hall, which cntertained a packed audience.

From here, Charlie went to Los Angeles, where the Oscar ceremony was to take place on April 11. On the day of the event, when Charlie peered through the backstage, he saw among the audience, some of his very old friends, who had all come to cheer him on his special day. After Taradash presented Charlie with the Oscar, he was asked to give a speech. Charlie was so overwhelmed by the long standing ovation which he received, that he could only manage these few words of appreciation, "Oh thank you so much...this is an emotional moment for me, and words are so futile, so feeble. I can only say that...thank you for inviting me here. And you're wonderful, sweet people."[262]

The next day, Charlie and his family returned to Europe. It had been a splendid tour, and all the grudges that Charlie had held against America for so long, were now slowly being washed away.

On Receiving Knighthood

In the meantime, Charlie's health had begun to fail. In his last public appearance, when he was receiving his Oscar, he had already started to look weak. He was unable to walk without greatly depending on his cane; that very cane, which had once made the walk of the tramp so memorable.

In 1975, when Charlie was awarded the Knighthood by Queen Elizabeth, he came into the hall, bound to a wheelchair. A newspaper article, written during that time, describes the ceremony as thus, "The band played Charlie Chaplin's theme music at Buckingham Palace today but it wasn't the little tramp with the funny walk who made his entrance before Queen Elizabeth but an old man in a wheel-chair. Bitterly disappointed that he could not kneel to be knighted as he had hoped, the great comedian bowed his head as the Queen tapped him on both the shoulders with a sword and dubbed him Sir Charles Chaplin.... Chaplin, 86 next month, clutched the order of knighthood, in its leather case, to his bosom as he stood at the exit of the palace, leaning heavily on a stick, and agreed that the positions were reversed.... Then he put his arm around his wife, who seemed surprised to be addressed as Lady Chaplin, and kissed her on both cheeks."[263]

His Last Breath

The news of the death of this great star was not sudden. During the last few years of his life, Charlie had been extremely happy. Having received awards and recognition, which were long due to him, he did not seem to have wanted anything else from life. He was content with his quiet and serene existence in Switzerland among his immediate family and friends.

Early morning at around four, on the day of the Christmas, December 25, 1977, when the whole house was decorated for the occasion, Charlie breathed his last. He was eighty-eight years old. It was a peaceful death, calm and quiet, and looked as if he was still sleeping. Seven of his children had been present in the house in Vevey on that day, except Geraldine, his eldest daughter, who was away for a film shooting. Oona was much distressed, and had told one of the newspapers, "All the presents were under the tree.... Charlie gave so much happiness and, although he had been ill for a long time, it is so sad that he should have passed away on Christmas day."[264]

The funeral of Charlie was a quiet affair, where only a few family members and close friends were present. He now lays buried in the Corsier Cemetery in Vevey.

A Small Incident Regarding His Coffin

Once about three years after Charlie's death, a couple of people had stolen his body from the grave and had held it for ransom. Nothing much came in the news about this incident, as the family decided to keep quiet about it. His coffin was finally found three months later, and was then re-buried in a vault, surrounded with cement.

One of the newspapers reported this episode as thus, "The coffin containing the body of Charlie Chaplin – missing since his grave was robbed 11 weeks ago – has been found. It was dug up from a field about a mile away from the Chaplin home in Corsier near Lausanne, Switzerland.... Swiss police have arrested two men...and say they have confessed to stealing the coffin and reburying it.... The family kept silent about the ransom demands and various rumours circulated about the missing coffin.... A spokesman for the Chaplins said, 'The family is very happy and relieved that the ordeal is over.'"[265]

The two thieves were then arrested and imprisoned for several years.

Weeping Willows

I've got the weeping willows
And I'm stepping through plate windows
On account of you
Oh my lord, what shall I do, what shall I do ?
I love you so
And yet I know you can't be true
If I only had a will to get away
But you have me in your spell both night and day
You have me in your power every moment, every hour
Leave me now or let me go
Why, oh why, torment me so ?
I despise you, idolise you, I adore you, I implore you
Let me be free
From this tyranny of love
I'm stepping through plate windows over you

[This was one of the songs which Charlie had written; it was featured in his movie A *King in New York* (1957).][266]

"He is the easiest man in the world to know but nobody knows him perhaps because of that fact. He has many eccentricities a reaction from the days when, as an ambitious artist, he yearned for something he couldn't have and then found, overnight, the world in his grasp. He is a man who has dreamed, and because his dreams came true, they embittered him."[267]

Nothing could have described Charlie better than these words, which were written by Douglas Fairbanks Jr., the son of Charlie's closest friend Douglas.

A mask of a comedian that he wore throughout his life, while inwardly suffering the various criticisms thrown upon him by the society, took a lot of courage. In the end, after having received his Oscar and Knighthood, it only felt that his story was complete, although he did not seem to have required them, as he was extremely pleased living alone with his family in Switzerland with no one to disturb him. The proof of this fact can be seen in the ending lines of his autobiography, which were written before America had realised his worth again, "For the last twenty years, I have known what happiness means.... As I live with Oona, the depth and beauty of her character are a continual revelation to me. Even as she walks ahead of me along the narrow sidewalks of Vevey with simple dignity, her neat little figure straight, her dark hair smoothed back showing a few silver threads, a sudden wave of love and admiration comes over me for all that she is – a lump comes into my throat. With such happiness, I sometimes sit out on our terrace at sunset and look over a vast green lawn to the lake in the distance, and beyond the lake to the reassuring mountains, and in this mood think of nothing but enjoy their magnificent serenity."[268]

His Achievements

Books

- *My Trip Abroad* (First published by Harper & Brothers, 1922)
- *A Comedian Sees the World* (1933)
- *My Autobiography* (1964)
- *My Life in Pictures* (1974)

Films

Keystone

1914

- Making a Living (1 reel)
- Kid Auto Races at Venice (split reel)

- Mabel's Strange Predicament (1 reel)
- Between Showers (1 reel)
- A Film Johnnie (1 reel)
- Tango Tangles (1 reel)
- His Favourite Pastime (1 reel)
- Cruel, Cruel Love (1 reel)
- The Star Boarder (1 reel)
- Mabel at the Wheel (2 reels)
- Twenty Minutes of Love (1 reel)
- Caught in a Cabaret (2 reels)
- Caught in the Rain (1 reel)
- A Busy Day (split reel)
- The Fatal Mallet (1 reel)
- Her Friend the Bandit (1 reel)
- The Knockout (2 reels)
- Mabel's Busy Day (1 reel)
- Mabel's Married Life (1 reel)
- Laughing Gas (1 reel)
- The Property Man (2 reels)
- The Face on the Bar-room Floor (1 reel)
- Recreation (split reel)
- The Masquerader (1 reel)
- His New Profession (1 reel)
- The Rounders (1 reel)
- The New Janitor (1 reel)
- Those Love Pangs (1 reel)
- Dough and Dynamite (2 reels)
- Gentleman of Nerve (1 reel)
- His Musical Career (1 reel)
- His Trysting Place (2 reels)
- Tillie's Punctured Romance (6 reels)
- Getting Acquainted (1 reel)
- His Prehistoric Past (2 reels)

Essanay

1915

- His New Job (2 reels)
- A Night Out (2 reels)
- The Champion (2 reels)
- In the Park (1 reel)
- The Jitney Elopement (2 reels)
- The Tramp (2 reels)
- By the Sea (1 reel)
- Work (2 reels)
- A Woman (2 reels)
- The Bank (2 reels)
- Shanghaied (2 reels)
- A Night in the Show (2 reels)

1916

- Carmen (4 reels)
- Police (2 reels)

1918

- Triple Trouble (2 reels)

Mutual

1916

- The Floorwalker (2 reels)
- The Fireman (2 reels)
- The Vagabond (2 reels)
- One a.m. (2 reels)
- The Count (2 reels)
- The Pawnshop (2 reels)
- Behind the Screen (2 reels)
- The Rink (2 reels)

1917

- Easy Street (2 reels)
- The Cure (2 reels)
- The Immigrant (2 reels)
- The Adventurer (2 reels)

First National

1918

- A Dog's Life (3 reels)
- The Bond (split reel)
- Shoulder Arms (3 reels)

1919

- Sunny Side (3 reels)
- A Day's Pleasure (2 reels)

1920

- The Kid (6 reels)
- The Idle Class (2 reels)

1922

- Pay Day (2 reels)

1923

- The Pilgrim (4 reels)

United Artists

Feature Films:

- A Woman of Paris (1923)
- The Gold Rush (1925)
- The Circus (1928)

- City Lights (1931)
- Modern Times (1936)
- The Great Dictator (1940)
- Monsieur Verdoux (1947)
- Limelight (1952)
- The King in New York (1957)

❑

Endnotes

1. Thomas Burke, "A Tragic Comedian: A close-up of Charles Chaplin", *The Outlook*, January 18, 1922.
2. John H. Butler, "Radio to Make Movies Talk", *Illustrated World*, July 1922, p. 673.
3. Charlie Chaplin, *My Autobiography*, "Introduction" by David Robinson.
4. Vaudeville is a genre of theatre which consists of various entertainment activities.
5. Charlie Chaplin, *My Autobiography*, (Melville House Publishing, 2012), p. 15.
6. Her maiden name was Smith and some biographers claim that she was his paternal grandmother, although in *My Autobiography* by Charlie Chaplin, it is not mentioned whether she was from his mother's side or father's.
7. W. Dodgson Bowman, *Charlie Chaplin: His Life and Art* (The John Day Company, New York), p. 11.
8. Charlie Chaplin, *My Autobiography*, p. 26.
9. *Ibid.*, pp. 40-41.
10. *Ibid.*, p. 33.
11. *Ibid.*, p. 35.
12. *Ibid.*, pp. 17-18.

13. *Ibid.*, p. 41.
14. *Ibid.*, p. 44.
15. *Ibid.*, pp. 45-46.
16. *Ibid.*, p. 62.
17. *Ibid.*, p. 66.
18. *Ibid.*, p. 70.
19. *Ibid.*, p. 74.
20. *Ibid.*, p. 91.
21. *Ibid.*, p. 93.
22. *Ibid.*, p. 95.
23. *Ibid.*, pp. 96-97.
24. *Ibid.*, p. 100.
25. W. Dodgson Bowman, *Charlie Chaplin: His Life and Art*, Chapter 3, "Charlie Discovers America", p. 34.
26. Charlie Chaplin, *My Autobiography*, pp. 120-121.
27. David Robinson, *Chaplin: His Life and Art*, (New York: McGraw-Hill Publishing Company), p. 82.
28. Charlie Chaplin, *My Autobiography*, pp. 135-136.
29. *Ibid.*, pp. 21-22.
30. *Ibid.*, p. 134.
31. Charles Chaplin Jr., *My Father, Charlie Chaplin*, (Random House, 1960), p. 240.
32. Charlie Chaplin, *My Autobiography*, p. 89.
33. *Ibid.*, p. 105.
34. *Ibid.*, p. 137.
35. John Kimber, *The Art of Charlie Chaplin*, Chapter 1 (Sheffield Academic Press, 2000), p. 14.
36. Charlie Chaplin, *My Autobiography*, pp. 145-146.
37. David Robinson, Charlie Chaplin — The Tramp who Conquered the World, January 8, 2010 article published by *London Evening Standard*.

38. Charlie Chaplin, *My Autobiography*, p. 150.
39. John Kimber, *The Art of Charlie Chaplin*, Chapter 2 (Sheffield Academic Press, 2000), p. 65.
40. Charlie Chaplin, *My Autobiography*, p. 146.
41. Mack Sennett and Cameron Shipp, *King of Comedy: The Lively Arts* (Garden City, NY, 1954), p. 180.
42. Charlie Chaplin, *My Autobiography*, p. 147.
43. *Ibid.*, p. 169.
44. John Kimber, *The Art of Charlie Chaplin*, Filmography (Sheffield Academic Press, 2000), p. 257.
45. Autumn Miller, "An Analysis of the Comedic Contributions of Charlie Chaplin", May 11, 2009 article published on the website of Yahoo.
46. Charlie Chaplin, *My Autobiography*, pp. 154-155.
47. Jeffrey Vance, Chaplin: Genius of the Cinema (New York, 2003) article published on the official website of Charlie Chaplin, www.charliechaplin.com; copyright 2009 Roy Export.
48. Charlie Chaplin, *My Autobiography*, p. 171.
49. *Ibid.*, pp. 174-175.
50. *Ibid.*, p. 174.
51. *Ibid.*, p. 178.
52. Autumn Miller, An Analysis of the Comedic Contributions of Charlie Chaplin, May 11, 2009 article published on the website of Yahoo.
53. Charlie Chaplin, *My Autobiography*, p. 47.
54. John Kimber, *The Art of Charlie Chaplin*, Chapter 3 (Sheffield Academic Press, 2000), pp. 77-85.
55. *Ibid.*, 93-101.
56. Charlie Chaplin, *My Autobiography*, p. 188.
57. John Kimber, *The Art of Charlie Chaplin*, Chapter 2 (Sheffield Academic Press, 2000), p. 53.

58. John Kimber, *The Art of Charlie Chaplin*, Chapter 4 (Sheffield Academic Press, 2000), pp. 107-113.
59. Charlie Chaplin, *My Autobiography*, p. 218.
60. John Kimber, *The Art of Charlie Chaplin*, Chapter 4 (Sheffield Academic Press, 2000), pp. 117-118.
61. Charlie Chaplin, *My Autobiography*, p. 224.
62. John Kimber, *The Art of Charlie Chaplin*, Chapter 4 (Sheffield Academic Press, 2000), p. 128.
63. Charlie Chaplin, *My Autobiography*, p. 232.
64. *Ibid.*, p. 269.
65. Alden Whitman, "Chaplin's Little Tramp, an Everyman Trying to Gild Cage of Life", *Enthralled World*, December 26, 1977 article published by *The New York Times*.
66. Charlie Chaplin, *My Autobiography*, p. 215.
67. *Ibid.*, p. 208.
68. *Ibid.*, p. 40.
69. *Ibid.*, p. 210.
70. Sergei Eisenstein was a pioneer in the use of the effect of 'montage'. His most popular movie was *Battleship Potemkin* (1925).
71. Charlie Chaplin, *My Autobiography*, p. 251.
72. *Ibid.*, p. 250.
73. *Ibid.*, p. 390.
74. *Ibid.*, p. 209.
75. *Ibid.*, p. 37.
76. *Ibid.*, p. 210.
77. *Ibid.*, p. 209.
78. *Ibid.*, p. 208.
79. John Kimber, *The Art of Charlie Chaplin*, Chapter 2 (Sheffield Academic Press, 2000), p. 57.
80. Charlie Chaplin, *My Autobiography*, p. 253.

81. *Ibid.*, p. 253.
82. *Ibid.*, p. 254.
83. *Ibid.*, p. 254.
84. Charlie Chaplin, *My Trip Abroad*, Chapter 1 (Harper & Brothers, 1922), p. 1.
85. David Robinson, *Chaplin: His Life and Art*, Chapter 8, "Escape" (Penguin Books, 2001).
86. Charlie Chaplin, *My Autobiography*, p. 264.
87. *Ibid.*, p. 279.
88. George Bernard Shaw was a celebrated author and playwright, known for his works, *Candida, Man and Superman, Caesar and Cleopatra* and others.
89. Charlie Chaplin, *My Autobiography*, p. 268.
90. Charlie Chaplin, *My Trip Abroad*, Chapter 10 (Harper & Brothers, 1922), p. 100.
91. Charlie Chaplin, *My Autobiography*, p. 271.
92. Charlie Chaplin, *My Trip Abroad*, Chapter 9 (Harper & Brothers, 1922), p. 89.
93. *Ibid.*, Chapter 10, p. 92.
94. *Ibid.*, Chapter 11, p. 105.
95. *Ibid.*, Chapter 11, pp. 107-108.
96. *Ibid.*, Chapter 12, p. 117.
97. *Ibid.*, Chapter 12, p. 114.
98. *Ibid.*, Chapter 13, p. 133.
99. John Kimber, *The Art of Charlie Chaplin*, Chapter 4 (Sheffield Academic Press, 2000), pp. 126-127.
100. Charlie Chaplin, *My Autobiography*, p. 221.
101. *Ibid.*, p. 221.
102. *Ibid.*, p. 294.
103. John Kimber, *The Art of Charlie Chaplin*, Chapter 5 (Sheffield Academic Press, 2000), p. 136.
104. Charlie Chaplin, *My Autobiography*, pp. 294-295.

105. *Ibid.*, p. 249.
106. *Ibid.*, p. 283-84.
107. *Ibid.*, p. 284.
108. *Ibid.*, p. 285.
109. Athletic Club was where Charlie lived for a long time.
110. Charlie Chaplin, *My Autobiography*, p. 226.
111. *Ibid.*, p. 228.
112. *Ibid.*, pp. 236-237.
113. *Ibid.*, p. 237.
114. *Ibid.*, p. 237.
115. *Ibid.*, p. 239.
116. *Ibid.*, p. 239.
117. *Ibid.*, p. 243.
118. *Ibid.*, p. 304.
119. *Ibid.*, p. 299.
120. *Ibid.*, p. 300.
121. John Kimber, *The Art of Charlie Chaplin*, Chapter 5 (Sheffield Academic Press, 2000), pp. 139-140.
122. David Robinson, "Filming the Gold Rush", 2004, MK2 article published in the official website of Charlie Chaplin (www.charliechaplin.com).
123. John Kimber, *The Art of Charlie Chaplin*, Chapter 5 (Sheffield Academic Press, 2000), pp. 149-151.
124. *Ibid.*, p. 144.
125. *Ibid.*, p. 153.
126. David Robinson, *"Filming the Circus"*, 2004, MK2 article published in the official website of Charlie Chaplin (www.charliechaplin.com).
127. *Ibid.*
128. John Kimber, *The Art of Charlie Chaplin*, Chapter 5 (Sheffield Academic Press, 2000), pp. 155-156.

129. *Ibid.*, pp. 160-61.
130. Charlie Chaplin, *My Autobiography*, pp. 285.
131. *Ibid.*, p. 286.
132. *Ibid.*, p. 287.
133. *Ibid.*, p. 287.
134. *Ibid.*, p. 316.
135. *Ibid.*, p. 317.
136. *Ibid.*, p. 320.
137. *Ibid.*, p. 321.
138. *Ibid.*, p. 321.
139. Tim Dirks, "The History of Film", article published on the website, www.filmsite.org.
140. *Filming City Lights*, David Robinson, 2004, MK2 article published in the official website of Charlie Chaplin (www.charliechaplin.com).
141. *Ibid.*
142. Charlie Chaplin, *My Autobiography*, p. 324.
143. John Kimber, *The Art of Charlie Chaplin*, Chapter 5 (Sheffield Academic Press, 2000), pp. 169-170.
144. *Ibid.*, p. 167.
145. Charlie Chaplin, *My Autobiography*, p. 324.
146. *Ibid.*, p. 326.
147. *Ibid.*, p. 327.
148. *Ibid.*, p. 332.
149. *Ibid.*, p. 333.
150. *Ibid.*, p. 334.
151. *Ibid.*, p. 336.
152. *Ibid.*, p. 337.
153. *Ibid.*, p. 343.
154. *Ibid.*, pp. 349-350.
155. *Ibid.*, p. 350.

156. *Ibid.*, p. 360.
157. *Ibid.*, p. 366.
158. *Ibid.*, p. 366.
159. *Ibid.*, p. 366.
160. *Ibid.*, p. 368.
161. Inukai Tsuyoshi, the then Prime Minister of Japan, was assassinated on May 15, 1932.
162. Charlie Chaplin, *My Autobiography*, p. 369.
163. Charlie Chaplin, *My Autobiography*, p. 369 quoted from *Government by Assassination* written by Hugh Byas.
164. New Deal was a series of economic reforms, which was devised by Franklin D. Roosevelt for the benefit of America.
165. Charlie Chaplin, *My Autobiography*, p. 374.
166. *Ibid.*, p. 377.
167. The lyrics of the song titled "Titine" sung by Charlie Chaplin in the movie *Modern Times* published in the official website of Charlie Chaplin, www.charliechaplin.com (1954, Bourne Co.).
168. John Kimber, *The Art of Charlie Chaplin*, Chapter 6 (Sheffield Academic Press, 2000), p. 98.
169. *Ibid.*, p. 184.
170. Charlie Chaplin, *My Autobiography*, p. 209.
171. David Robinson, "Filming Modern Times", 2004, MK2 article published in the official website of Charlie Chaplin (www.charliechaplin.com).
172. Charlie Chaplin, *My Autobiography*, p. 378.
173. *Ibid.*, p. 375.
174. *Ibid.*, p. 375.
175. Samuel Goldwyn was a part of MGM (Metro-Goldwyn-Mayer).
176. Charlie Chaplin, *My Autobiography*, p. 377.
177. *Ibid.*, p. 400.

178. *The Gamine: Paulette Goddard*, contributed by Garen Ewing published in the official website of Charlie Chaplin, www.charliechaplin.com
179. Charlie Chaplin, *My Autobiography*, p. 296.
180. *Ibid.*, p. 297.
181. *Ibid.*, p. 354.
182. Cornelius Vanderbilt's accounts on Hitler resulted in the production of a docu-drama, *Hitler's Reign of Terror*, which was released in 1934.
183. Charlie Chaplin, *My Autobiography*, p. 316.
184. *Ibid.*, p. 387-88.
185. *Ibid.*, p. 386.
186. Christian Delage, *Chaplin Facing History* (Jean Michel Place, 2005). It was a remark made by Charlie Chaplin.
187. Charlie Chaplin, *My Autobiography*, p. 387.
188. *Ibid.*, p. 387.
189. *Ibid.*, p. 389.
190. *Ibid.*, p. 386.
191. *Ibid.*, p. 393.
192. John Kimber, *The Art of Charlie Chaplin*, Chapter 6, (Sheffield Academic Press, 2000), pp. 206-08.
193. *Ibid.*, p. 205.
194. *Ibid.*, p. 210.
195. The ending speech from *The Great Dictator* (1940) written and carried out by Charlie Chaplin.
196. Charlie Chaplin, *My Autobiography*, p. 254.
197. *Ibid.*, p. 393.
198. *Ibid.*, p. 402-403.
199. *To support the President's Rally for a Second Front Now*, Madison Square Park, July 22, 1942 speech published in *My Autobiography*, Charlie Chaplin, pp. 405-06.
200. Charlie Chaplin, *My Autobiography*, p. 411.

201. *Chaplin and American Culture: The Evolution of a Star Image* by Charles J. Maland.
202. Charlie Chaplin, *My Autobiography*, p. 407.
203. *Ibid.*, p. 409.
204. *Chaplin and American Culture: The Evolution of a Star Image* by Charles J. Maland.
205. *Ibid.*
206. Charlie Chaplin, *My Autobiography*, p. 415.
207. *Ibid.*, p. 417.
208. *Ibid.*, p. 417.
209. *Ibid.*, p. 422.
210. *Ibid.*, p. 425.
211. *Ibid.*, p. 414.
212. *Ibid.*, p. 414.
213. A small village near Santa Barbara.
214. They married in June 1943.
215. Charlie Chaplin, *My Autobiography*, p. 415-416.
216. *Ibid.*, p. 416.
217. A breed of dog.
218. Charlie Chaplin, *My Autobiography*, p. 426.
219. David Robinson, "Filming Monsieur Verdoux", 2004, MK2 article published in the official website of Charlie Chaplin (www.charliechaplin.com).
220. Charlie Chaplin, *My Autobiography*, p. 429.
221. *Ibid.*, p. 444.
222. John Kimber, *The Art of Charlie Chaplin*, Chapter 6 (Sheffield Academic Press, 2000), p. 216.
223. David Robinson, "Filming Monsieur Verdoux", 2004, MK2 article published in the official website of Charlie Chaplin (www.charliechaplin.com).
224. Charlie Chaplin, *My Autobiography*, p. 443.
225. *Ibid.*, p. 442.

226. David Robinson, "Filming Monsieur Verdoux", 2004, MK2 article published in the official website of Charlie Chaplin (www.charliechaplin.com).
227. Charlie Chaplin, *My Autobiography*, p. 441.
228. *Ibid.*, p. 445.
229. *Ibid.*, p. 439.
230. David Robinson, "Filming Limelight", 2004, MK2 article published in the official website of Charlie Chaplin (www.charliechaplin.com).
231. Charlie Chaplin, *My Autobiography*, p. 257.
232. Melissa Hayden and André Eglevsky were the choreographers of the movie.
233. Charlie Chaplin, *My Autobiography*, p. 447.
234. John Kimber, *The Art of Charlie Chaplin*, Chapter 6 (Sheffield Academic Press, 2000), p. 179.
235. Charlie Chaplin, *My Autobiography*, p. 449.
236. *Ibid.*, p. 452.
237. *Ibid.*, p. 454.
238. *Ibid.*, p. 455.
239. J. Edgar Hoover was appointed as the Director of Bureau of Investigation (from which FBI was formed) in 1924. He held this position till he died in 1972.
240. Charlie Chaplin, *My Autobiography*, p. 455.
241. *Ibid.*, p. 457.
242. *Ibid.*, p. 458.
243. *Ibid.*, p. 458.
244. *Ibid.*, p. 458.
245. *Ibid.*, p. 461-462.
246. *Ibid.*, p. 464.
247. *Ibid.*, p. 464.
248. *Ibid.*, p. 463.
249. *Ibid.*, p. 465.

250. *Ibid.*, pp. 469-470.
251. *Ibid.*, p. 475.
252. *Ibid.*, p. 473.
253. *Ibid.*, p. 473.
254. *Ibid.*, p. 470.
255. *Ibid.*, p. 472.
256. "Filming a King in New York", article published in the official website of Charlie Chaplin (www.charliechaplin.com).
257. Joseph McCarthy, Senator of Wisconsin (1947-57), carried out anti-communist activities, which led to the creation of the term 'McCarthyism'.
258. *Chaplin and American Culture: The Evolution of a Star Image* by Charles J. Maland.
259. *Ibid.*
260. *Ibid.*
261. *Ibid.*
262. Transcribed from the YouTube video of Charlie Chaplin receiving his Oscar.
263. *Sad Charlie Chaplin knighted in London*, Robert Musel, 'The Register Guard', Eugene, March 4, 1975.
264. *Charlie Chaplin Dead at 88, Made the Film an Art Form*, Bosley Crowther, *"The New York Times"*, December 26, 1977.
265. *Charlie Chaplin's stolen body found*, May 17, 1978 Report published on the website of BBC News, news.bbc.co.uk
266. Published on the official website of Charlie Chaplin, www.charliechaplin.com. Copyright belongs to Bourne Co.
267. W. Dodgson Bowman, *Charlie Chaplin: His Life and Art*, 'Introduction' (The John Day Company, New York).
268. Charlie Chaplin, *My Autobiography*, p. 477.

❑❑❑